ANTI BULLYING ACTION

Dr Allan Beane

Introduction by Molly Potter

100+ Practical Ideas and Activities for the Primary Classroom

A & C Black • London

Published in association with

First published in the UK in 2008 by
A & C Black Publishers Ltd
38 Soho Square
London W1D 3HB
www.acblack.com

Additional text by Molly Potter
Kidscape editor: Catherine Calvert

ISBN: 978-1-4081-0476-7

12 11 10 09 08
10 9 8 7 6 5 4 3 2 1

Printed by: Caligraving Ltd, Thetford, Norfolk
Index by: Indexing Specialists (UK) Ltd
Cover illustration by: KJA-Artists.com

A & C Black uses paper produced with
elemental chlorine-free pulp, harvested from
mmanaged, sustainable forests.

DEDICATION

This book is dedicated to my wife, Linda, for her unconditional love and support throughout the writing of this book, and to my son and daughter, Curtis and Christy Beane, for their shared experiences and insights regarding the importance of peer acceptance.

Dr Allan Beane

ABOUT THE AUTHORS

Allan L. Beane Ph.D., is a nationally recognised expert, speaker and author on bullying in the USA. A former classroom teacher, he develops bullying prevention programmes for schools and is a sought-after speaker on the topic. He also offers expert support to those who deal with school violence.

Molly Potter has taught for 11 years and now works as a SRE (Sex and Relationships Education) Development Worker supporting Norfolk primary schools in the development of their SRE programme and policy.

Contents

Photocopiable pages

Introduction

Anyone who believes in developing and preserving children's self-worth and confidence will know that bullying is not acceptable. Children and young people have the right to feel safe, secure, accepted and valued and be free from teasing, name-calling, threats, violence and fear. Preserving these rights is fundamental to anti-bullying.

There has been a significant focus on bullying in recent years and research into its prevalence clarifies that it is a significant and serious problem. Around one in four primary school children and one in three secondary school children are bullied at some point in their school life. Research also highlights the fact that a lot of bullying still remains unreported.

The long- and short-term damage of bullying is well documented. For targets it can cause stress, illness, reduced self-esteem, an inhibited ability to make friends, reduced academic achievement, withdrawal, and in the most extreme cases, suicide. The effects of bullying can be far-reaching. Some adults have reported still feeling angry about being bullied as a child and that it has had a knock-on effect throughout their lives. Extreme bullies themselves can become bullying adults. Bullying is learned behaviour and bullies need to be taught better ways of relating to others. All in all bullying means suffering and this is undisputed.

Tackling bullying is not just about dealing with children that bully – although clear actions that demonstrate that bullying is totally unacceptable undoubtedly have an impact. With bullying, prevention is just as important as intervention. Children need to develop empathy for others and the skills needed for successful relationships (including effective communication) if bullying is to be fully addressed. Furthermore, if these skills are developed the benefits become more than just a reduction in bullying. An anti-bullying school is likely to be a school where positive relationships and interactions are enhanced.

What is bullying?

The Department for Children, Schools and Families (DCSF) defines bullying as:

Behaviour by an individual or group, usually repeated over time, that intentionally hurts another individual or group either physically or emotionally.

From *Safe to learn: Embedding anti-bullying work in schools. DCFS 00656-2007*

Headteachers have a legal duty to draw up procedures to prevent bullying among pupils and to bring these procedures to the attention of staff, parents and pupils.

AN ANTI-BULLYING SCHOOL

So what does a school that has accepted the responsibility of anti-bullying look like? For a start, it has fully acknowledged that bullying does happen and fully understands its potentially devastating effects. It uses this understanding when drawing up an anti-bullying policy – the process of which involves the whole school community: parents/carers, pupils, all school staff and possibly key members from the local community and external agencies. Everyone who is involved in the policy development is clear about what bullying is because time is dedicated to defining it.

The policy development and related activities mean that the school is developing a strong anti-bullying ethos. All adults in the school follow and demonstrate anti-bullying behaviour and procedures. There is a culture of reporting any bullying incident and all staff, pupils and parents look out for signs of it. Pupils feel listened to when they tell adults about bullying. Every incident is taken seriously and there are very clear procedures for reporting, dealing with (including sanctions and

---

* (SOURCE: BBC News 22 November 2004)

support for the bully and support for the targets) and monitoring bullying incidents. All bullying incidents are followed up to watch out for recurrence.

In this school, the curriculum (particularly PSHE and/or SEAL) also strongly supports anti-bullying messages and promotes positive behaviours. Pupils have many opportunities to learn social skills, positive communication (including assertiveness) and to develop their self-esteem through an encouraging class and school environment. Each year in anti-bullying week, pupils are reminded about what bullying is, what a person should do if they are being bullied and what they should do if they witness bullying. Anti-bullying and positive behaviour are celebrated regularly in whole-school assemblies.

This school prioritises all of its anti-bullying work. The headteacher takes his/her role of monitoring bullying in the school seriously. He/she also taps into the anti-bullying support offered by the local authority. The school reviews its policy once every two years. This review involves the whole school community each time. The policy has strong links to other school policies. A child-friendly version of the anti-bullying policy has also been written by the Year 6 pupils as yet another means of ensuring all pupils know what to do about this issue.

As a result of the effort dedicated to anti-bullying, pupils report that they feel safe at school, that they believe that no one deserves to be bullied and that bullying is unacceptable. Furthermore, pupils generally build strong friendships and bullying has been significantly reduced.

SO WHERE DOES THIS BOOK COME IN?

Anti-Bullying Action provides school staff with a collection of tips, strategies and activities designed to address the multi-faceted problem of bullying in schools. It places equal emphasis on prevention and intervention as it includes activities that are suitable for:

- use with whole classes – enhancing positive interactions and increasing awareness of bullying

- use with pupils who have been identified as vulnerable to bullying and

- pupils who do, or are likely to, bully.

Using this book will provide your pupils with positive experiences that aim to raise awareness of bullying and reduce the likelihood of it happening. The activities in this book can positively contribute to a whole-school approach to anti-bullying.

HOW TO USE THIS BOOK

Anti-Bullying Action is not a complete programme and it is certainly not intended that a teacher works through it in order or completes every activity. *Anti-Bullying Action* contains a range of activities and a range of approaches and it is unlikely that every activity would be suitable for all classes. Many activities stand alone (although some do have a suggested sequence) and this is a resource to be dipped into.

Anti-Bullying Action can be used:

- to enhance the SEAL curriculum 'Say No to bullying' theme

- to provide purposeful activities in your school during anti-bullying week

- to address a particular positive behaviour or anti-bullying issue in your class or school

- to develop your own anti-bullying module as part of the PSHE curriculum

- for dealing with individuals involved in bullying (including targets).

It is advisable that you choose what to use from this book with due consideration, adapting and evaluating each activity or combination of activities to meet the specific needs of your class. You might also consider that some activities need 'aging up' or 'aging down'.

Some activities are simple and take moments; others take longer and can be more involved. Most activities are quick to understand and implement and need little or no advance preparation with little or no special equipment.

The suggestions labelled 'Go further' are for extending an activity or exploring an issue in greater depth. Some activities are linked with a 'see also' label because of their relevant links – especially as some activities would be just as appropriate for targets as for bullies because of the complex nature of bullying. There are also photocopiable worksheets for use with many of the activities.

HOW THE BOOK IS ORGANISED

The main part of *Anti-Bullying Action* is split into three sections for ease of use:

CREATING A POSITIVE CLASSROOM (page 16)
This section, ideal for whole-class use, includes many tips, strategies and techniques designed to change everyone's attitudes and behaviours for the better. These activities are a good place to start because they help to set the scene and give everyone a shared language and understanding of bullying.

HELPING TARGETS (page 81)
This section provides intervention strategies for use with pupils who are, or are likely to become, targets. They can be used by class teachers but might be more effectively used by Special Educational Needs Coordinators (SENCOs) or Teaching Assistants (TAs) with small groups of pupils who have been identified as having an increased likelihood of being a target of bullying. To identify such pupils a list of warning signs can be found on pages 83–84.

HELPING BULLIES (pages 113)
This section includes ideas for turning around the behaviour of bullies. They need help as much as targets do. Like the activities in the last section, these could be used by a class teacher or by SENCOs or TAs with small groups of pupils who have been identified as having an increased likelihood of exhibiting bullying behaviour. To identify such pupils a list of warning signs can be found on pages 118–119.

BACKGROUND READING

If a teacher wishes to develop an in-depth understanding of bullying and how to prevent it, a good place to start would be 'The Top Ten Facts About Bullying' in the next section of this book. Further resources can be found listed in the back of this book.

Keeping parents/carers involved

A vital part of anti-bullying work is involving parents and carers so that they are informed about bullying and the measures that are taken to prevent and intervene with it. Keeping everyone in the loop helps to make anti-bullying messages more consistent and therefore more effective.

On page 4 you will find a letter that could be used or adapted for use to introduce the anti-bullying work you will be doing with your class.

Other very useful resources that can be shared with parents can be found on pages 94–96, 'Helping children to combat bullying' and pages 121–122 'Bringing out the best in children'.

Dear Parent / Caregiver,

As I look back on my school days, I can remember times when children were bullied. You probably can, too. Bullying has been getting a lot of attention recently, but it's hardly a brand-new problem. Bullies (and their targets) have been around forever.

What's new is our attitude towards bullying. What used to be accepted as "children will be children" (or "boys will be boys", though girls are bullies, too) has changed. We know now that bullying is serious. Young bullies can grow up to be abusive adults. Young targets get hurt. Bullying can escalate into violence. And it's not just the bullies and targets who are affected. People around them are distracted, intimidated and upset. Bullying in the classroom prevents children from learning and teachers from teaching.

What's also new is our commitment to do something about bullying. If it's not a problem, we want to make sure it doesn't start. That's called prevention. If it is a problem, we're determined to stop it. That's called intervention.

As your child's teacher, I'm committed to prevention and intervention in my classroom, creating a positive environment where everyone feels safe, accepted and valued.

From time to time, I'll send home materials related to what we're doing in the classroom, and your child may tell you about some of the activities and discussions that are happening in class. If you ever have questions or concerns, I hope you'll contact me personally.

Sincerely,

_____

(Name)

_____

(Telephone)

The top ten facts about bullying

This section provides a broad, general overview of what bullying is, who is affected by bullying, and why it's important for teachers and parents to get involved in prevention and intervention. You might read this before you jump into the main sections of this book, then refer to it periodically for answers, insights and inspiration as you work with your pupils to create an anti-bullying classroom.

1. BULLYING IS NOT JUST ABOUT PHYSICAL VIOLENCE

The stereotypical image of bullying is a large, thug-like male hitting a smaller, 'swotty' looking male. This does not represent the full scope of bullying that exists and can perpetuate an idea that could prevent different versions of bullying from being taken seriously and addressed.

The DCSF defines bullying as:

Behaviour by an individual or group, usually repeated over time, that intentionally hurts another individual or group either physically or emotionally.

From *Safe to learn: Embedding anti-bullying work in schools.* DCSF 00656-2007

Bullying can be physical (e.g. punching, kicking, unwanted sexual contact, spitting, shoving or any form of violence) but it can also be emotional (e.g. ostracising someone, teasing and taunting, graffiti, cyber bullying – nasty text messages, use of websites and chat rooms to be vindictive towards others, making rude gestures, spreading rumours, homophobic comments, damaging or hiding someone's property or racist comments). Both types of bullying can seriously damage a person's confidence and self-worth and need to be given equal rank in seriousness.

2. ANYONE CAN BE A BULLY

Bullies are people who need to feel powerful, and they have learned that bullying works. What distinguishes them from someone who teases occasionally is a pattern of *repeated* physical or psychological intimidation.

There is no one reason why a child may become a bully, but environmental factors can lead to the development of bullying behaviours. Because this behaviour is learned, it can also be unlearned. The pattern of behaviour can begin as early as age two; the older the child becomes with bullying behaviours unchallenged, the more difficult change will be. Child bullies are at a greater risk for problems in the future. In one study, by age thirty, 25 per cent of the adults who had been identified as bullies as children had a criminal record, as opposed to 5 per cent of the adults who hadn't been bullies.*

Some environmental factors that contribute to the development of bullying behaviour include the following:**

- *Too little supervision of children and adolescents.* Children need to get the message that bullying behaviour is not okay.

- A *'payoff'*. When parents or other adults give in to an obnoxious or aggressive child, the

* (SOURCE: *Bullies and Victims* by SuEllen Fried, ADTR, and Paula Fried, PhD (New York: M. Evans and Company, 1994) Early intervention is essential.

** (SOURCE: Bullying Fact Sheet by George Batsche and Benjamin Moore, in *Helping Children Grow Up in the '90s: A Resource Book for Parents and Teachers* (Bethesda, MD: National Association of School Psychologists, 1992). Used with permission.

child learns to use bullying to get what he or she wants.

- *Aggressive behaviour in the home.* Some children are more likely than others to imitate aggressive behaviour. Watching adults bully each other gives children the tools they need to become bullies themselves.

- *Harsh physical punishment.* Some bullies often attack smaller, weaker children to model what happens to them in their homes. The worst possible punishment for bullies is physical.

- *Abusive peers.* Children may be bullied by their 'friends' or may be encouraged to bully to be part of the group.

- *Constant negative feedback.* Bullies feel that the world around them is more negative than positive. As a result, they use negative behaviour to feel important and get attention.

- *Expecting hostility.* In many ways, the bully's philosophy is "the best defence is offence". They attack before they are attacked, and assume hostility where none may exist.

3. ANYONE CAN BE A TARGET AND TARGETS NEED SUPPORT

In general, less is known about targets than about bullies. There are generalisations that can be made about targets but there are always exceptions to these. Children can be victimised because of their physical appearance, race, religion, abilities, sexuality, mannerisms, or just because they don't appear to fit in. In fact, one survey shows that 'not fitting in' is the most common reason why a child is abused by peers.* Children who have a disability or a chronic illness are common targets. Other targets are the children of overly protective or domineering parents/carers. It is also true to say that in some cases there is no discernible reason why a child becomes a target of bullying.

* (SOURCE: *The Bullying Prevention Handbook* by John H. Hoover and Ronald Oliver (Bloomington, IN: National Education Service, 1996)

Many targets are either *passive* (anxious, insecure etc.) or *provocative* (hot-tempered, restless etc.). Provocative targets are also at risk of becoming bullies themselves. A few children who are victimised don't fit either category – talented or popular children are also victimised. Some pupils see high achievers as 'sucking up' to teachers and decide to torment them into changing their behaviours. Of course, this kind of bullying may be based on jealousy.

Research shows that children who are frequently victimised are more likely to 'reward' bullies physically or emotionally (by giving up their lunch money or bursting into tears, for example) and less likely to fight back.

It is extremely important when dealing with targets of bullying, that there is never any insinuation of the bullying being deserved. Although positive and worthwhile steps can be taken to reduce the likelihood of an individual being bullied, the ultimate responsibility for intervening and stopping the bullying lies with the adults in that child's life – after all, a bullying situation would not arise if the child could sort out the situation by themselves.

Targets need protection from the negative impact of bullying. In the short term, they may feel afraid and lonely and often attempt to avoid situations in which they may be bullied. In the long term, children who are victimised begin to see themselves as unworthy or inferior, and their academic performance suffers. Some children eventually believe that they deserve the abuse; this phenomenon is also common in targets of domestic abuse. Over time, a victimised person can develop a target mentality as a permanent part of his or her psyche. This type of target needs help from a professional therapist or counsellor.

Victimised children are also at a greater risk for depression and suicide than their non-bullied peers. They may, in extreme cases, see suicide as their only way to escape.

4. BULLYING ISN'T A MODERN PROBLEM

Bullying in schools is nothing new. In the 1850s novel *Tom Brown's Schooldays*, author Thomas Hughes vividly described how a younger boy at an English boarding school was forced by a group of older bullies to undergo a painful and sadistic roasting in front of an open fire.*

Other literary references to bullying throughout history are plentiful although often it is extreme cases of violent bullying that are portrayed – as historically, verbal and emotional abuse was not considered to actually be bullying.

Unfortunately, adults have been relatively slow to protect the rights of children. Corporal punishment was banned in state schools as late as 1986. This was not extended to all schools until 1998. It could be argued that this showed a mind-set that it was reasonable for adults to bully children up until relatively recently, and the idea that children needed to be protected from bullying by other children would certainly not have been ubiquitous.

It was only in the latter part of the 1980s that bullying started to be taken seriously in the UK. Legislation and guidance has recently been plentiful but the change in attitude towards the seriousness of bullying has not been immediate.

Bullying can be put to rest only when it is recognised and steps are taken to prevent it. Ignoring the problem will not make it go away.

5. BULLYING AFFECTS EVERYONE

If bullying goes unchallenged, bullies do not get the opportunity to develop better ways of interacting with others and continue to bully, and targets remain unable to defend themselves and are often seriously affected. Another, less obvious impact is that on the witnesses of bullying.

Children who watch other children being bullied are often afraid to speak out, perhaps thinking "That could be me!" A child who is victimised may be rejected by his or her peers as if the target had some sort of disease. (One common variation of this is the childhood game in which one child has 'fleas' that he or she attempts to pass on to others.) Some children who witness a great deal of bullying react as many targets do – they attempt to avoid the situation and may even develop headaches, stomach aches or other physical symptoms of stress. An atmosphere where children worry "who will be next" encourages absences, truancy and dropping out of school.

Studies with English and Australian schoolchildren and adolescents showed that most students were opposed to bullying and tended to be supportive of targets. Half tried to help targets, and nearly one-third regretted not helping.

However, children become less sympathetic to targets as they grow older; almost one-third of the adolescents surveyed said they could understand why the bully chose the target.

In a US study, children aged about 9 to 12 were asked to imagine aggressive acts against targets and non-targets. In their minds, hurting the targets was less upsetting than hurting the non-targets.*

Blaming the target is a common reaction among children. Like many adults, children may believe that bad things don't happen to good people, so the target must be doing something wrong to deserve the abuse. They may also feel that the abuse makes the target 'tougher'. These attitudes help them justify their inaction.

Not every child, of course, ignores the mistreatment of their peers, but intervention can have a high cost if a young person's safety is not protected when they report bullying. In England, a 16-year-old girl who went to the police and identified one of a group of 20 boys who had severely beaten a Pakistani student was both praised and vilified. In the year after the incident, she received death threats, was verbally abused by total strangers,

* (SOURCE: *Set Straight on Bullies* by Stuart Greenbaum with Brenda Turner and Ronald D. Stephens (Malibu, CA: National School Safety Center, 1989)

* (SOURCE: *Childhood Bullying and Teasing* by Dorothea M. Ross, PhD (Alexandria, VA: American Counseling Association, 1996)

was bullied at school, and suffered a concussion and minor injuries when she was attacked by another student.* This example, although extreme and rare, highlights the need for the intolerance of bullying to be a far more prevalent concept and one that children and adults alike have completely bought into.

6. BULLYING IS A SERIOUS AND PREVALENT PROBLEM

The law protects adults against crimes like theft, extortion, slander and assault and battery. An adult who throws rocks and shouts obscenities at another adult will probably be arrested. This protection should extend equally to children, who generally are considered more vulnerable and less able to defend themselves. Unfortunately, this isn't always the case. It is generally understood that bullying – including violent bullying of others – is still under-reported.

According to Dr Dan Olweus, one of the world's leading authorities on bullying, "a person is being bullied or victimised when he or she is exposed, repeatedly and over time, to negative actions on the part of one or more persons." This *repeated* nature is the most disturbing aspect of bullying according to some researchers. Bullying is a consistent pattern of disrespect for others, accepted and even created by the environment.

This might explain the popularity of television shows in which children watch people falling down, getting hit by planks of wood or bitten by dogs. The laughter of others convinces them that these things are funny. Pupils who become bullies don't see their targets as people and can't see the consequences of their own actions.

Many bullies often object to being disciplined, claiming "We were just having fun." The difference between playful teasing, hurtful teasing, bullying and abuse is not always clear. Because much of the pain of being victimised is emotional or social, it is less evident than a cut or a bruise. A pupil can

be in a great deal of pain without having a visible injury. Words can hurt, and verbal abuse can lead to physical abuse with frightening ease. This is why it is so important for children and young people to fully understand what bullying is as well as its impact.

It is hard to get reliable statistics about bullying and any investigation on the Internet will give varied results. However, to get some idea of the prevalence and seriousness of bullying, here are a few statistics from reliable sources.

- The helpline Childline took more than 30,000 calls about bullying last year – a quarter of its total.

- More 12-year-olds call Childline about bullying than any other age group.

- Over half of primary and secondary school pupils (51 per cent and 54 per cent, respectively) thought that bullying was a "big problem" or "quite a problem" in their school.*

- Around one in four primary school children and one in three secondary school children are bullied at some point in their school life, according to official estimates.**

- One in ten primary aged pupils are persistently and frequently bullied – possibly every day.***

- Studies claim that at least 16 children commit suicide as a direct result of bullying every year in the UK.****

---

* (SOURCE: Summary report of DfES 2003 – *Tackling bullying and DfES anti-bullying pack for schools, 2003*)

** (SOURCE: BBC News 22 November 2004)

*** (SOURCE: Presentation from Sonia Sharp, Director of Children and Young People's Services in a presentation to the DCSF)

**** (SOURCE: *Bullycide, Death at Playtime* by Neil Marr and Tim Field, 2001)

---

* (SOURCE *Childhood Bullying and Teasing* by Dorothea M. Ross, PhD (Alexandria, VA: American Counseling Association, 1996)

7. HELPING EVERYONE TO DEAL WITH CONFLICT POSITIVELY WILL IMPACT ON BULLYING

Simply enrolling a target in a karate class is not the answer. Because bullying has a variety of causes, we need to find a variety of ways of dealing with it.

Obviously, many situations in which bullying occurs involve some sort of conflict. Young people (and their adult role models) need to learn conflict management and resolution skills, which can help stop these bullying problems from developing.

Schools can create an atmosphere where healthy choice-making is encouraged. This version of 'the three R's' can make a difference in the school environment:*

- *Rules*. Parents and school personnel must demonstrate that they are in charge and won't tolerate any pupil hurting another pupil, either physically or psychologically. Clear boundaries need to be set so that children and young people clearly know what is and what is not acceptable.

- *Rights*. Every pupil has the right not to be hurt and the right to learn in a safe environment.

- *Responsibilities*. Educators must be responsible for better supervision and more observant monitoring. By eliminating fear from the lives of pupils, teachers are able to do their jobs more effectively. Also, pupils must be responsible for respecting the rights of their classmates and themselves.

The involvement of parents, teachers, all other school staff, pupils, and the community is essential in stopping bullying in schools. Research on school climate suggests that the headteacher is the single most important person to have involved in anti-bullying work. School staff will follow the lead of an effective, motivated headteacher.* The larger the group of concerned and involved parents, teachers, pupils and community members, the better off the school will be.

In peer mediation, all pupils (or just a few, depending on the model) are trained to help pupils work out their differences by leading them through a series of steps or an outline. Here's one example of a series of mediation steps:

- *Relax*. **Take a step back from the problem and admit how you feel.**

- *Choose to solve the problem*. **Let the other person know that you are ready to talk things through. Stay calm and don't do anything to make the problem worse.**

- *Share your feelings*. **Talk about the situation using 'I statements' (e.g. I felt awful when...). Be honest and specific about your feelings. Answer any questions the other person might have.**

- *Listen*. **Without interrupting, listen to the other person's point of view. When the other person is finished, you can ask a few more questions to find out more. Keep the questions simple.**

- *Find a solution*. **Together, agree on a way to solve the problem. Then put the plan into action.**

- *Make a plan for the future*. **Think of some better ways to handle the situation if it happens again. Agree to try one of these ideas next time.**

Many modern conflict resolution programmes stress peer mediation, a concept found in many cultures. In ancient China, people practised the Confucian way of resolving disputes by using moral persuasion and agreement. In Japan, the village leader was expected to use mediation and conciliation to help community members settle their disputes. In parts of Africa, a neighbourhood meeting, or 'moot', assembled, and a respected

---

* (SOURCE: *Set Straight on Bullies* by Stuart Greenbaum with Brenda Turner and Ronald D. Stephens (Malibu, CA: National School Safety Center, 1989, http://www.nssc1.org) Used with permission

* (SOURCE: *The Bullying Prevention Handbook* by John H. Hoover and Ronald Oliver (Bloomington, IN: National Education Service, 1996)

member helped disputants resolve their conflict without involving a judge.*

Holocaust survivor Victor Frankl saw the importance of taking responsibility for our own actions when he said, "Everything can be taken from us but one thing, which is the last of the human freedoms – to choose one's attitude in any given set of circumstances, to choose one's own way."

People who solve problems without resorting to violence seldom make the evening news. Getting along just isn't that exciting. But learning conflict resolution skills can increase a child's EQ ('emotional quotient'), which some experts claim is as essential to success as IQ. Assertiveness training, self esteem and self awareness development, and a consistent, organised approach to discipline are other important aspects that should be included in a bullying prevention plan. Concerned adults can make a difference.

8. ANTI-BULLYING NEEDS TIME AND THOUGHT DEVOTED TO IT

An effective bullying prevention programme and anti-bullying policy will include short-term actions and activities that relate to long-term goals. Identifying specific areas for action helps schools to recognise and address overlapping goals, conflicting messages and missed opportunities.

In considering its approach to anti-bullying, a school could reflect upon the checklist on pages 11–12.

Further suggestions include:

- Establish zero tolerance policies for violence. Spell out sanctions in advance. Adopt the motto "If it's illegal outside school, it's illegal inside." Educate pupils, parents and staff about policies and sanctions. Include a way for pupils to report bully-related information that does not expose them to retaliation.

- Establish a committee (including pupils) to develop a safe school plan. Policies need to include procedures for both day-to-day operations and crisis handling and could cover such subjects as identifying who belongs in the building, avoiding accidents and incidents in corridors and on school grounds, reporting any 'weapons' or anything that could potentially cause harm, working in partnership with police, and following up to ensure that troubled pupils get help.

- Offer training in anger management, stress relief, mediation, and related violence prevention skills to staff and teachers. Help them identify ways to pass these skills along to pupils. Make sure pupils are getting training.

- Adopt a whole school community approach – involve parents/carers, all school staff, visiting staff, any support offered from the local authority and any relevant members of the local community in setting up solutions to violence and bullying. Keep lines of communication open to all.

- Develop ways to make it easier for parents/carers to be involved. Provide lists of volunteer opportunities; ask parents/carers to organise phone trees for emergencies; hold events on weekends as well as weeknights. Offer child care for younger children.

- Work with community groups and police to create safe routes for travel to and from school. Help with efforts to identify and eliminate trouble spots in the neighbourhood.

- Reward good behaviour. Acknowledging pupils who do the right thing – whether it's settling an argument without violence, helping another pupil, or apologising for bumping into someone – helps raise the tone for the whole school.

- Insist that your staff treat each other and pupils the way they want to be treated – with respect, courtesy, and thoughtfulness. Be the chief role model.

---

* (SOURCE: *Reducing School Violence Through Conflict Resolution* by Davis W. Johnson and Robert T. Johnson (Alexandria, VA: ASCD, 1995)

Issue	Points for consideration
Priority	• Is the issue of bullying taken seriously by the leadership in the school?
School ethos	• Are positive behaviours demonstrated and celebrated by the school staff? • Is the school's commitment to zero tolerance to bullying obvious? • Does the school prospectus reflect both the expectation of positive behaviour and zero tolerance to negative behaviour? • Is the school inclusive and does it celebrate diversity?
Policies	• Is the anti-bullying policy a working document? • Were all school staff, pupils, parents/carers and other members of the community consulted about the policy and made aware of its contents? • Is the anti-bullying policy reviewed at least once every two years? • Do all policies reflect a consistent approach to behaviour and bullying?
Planning	• Does anti-bullying feature significantly in the school Self-Evaluation Form? • Is time regularly devoted to the anti-bullying agenda?
Curriculum/Prevention	• Are anti-bullying and positive behaviour assemblies held regularly? • Does the school acknowledge anti-bullying week? • Do pupils receive regular reminders about bullying through the curriculum (including what bullying is, how it affects others, what can be done about bullying and how bullying is totally unacceptable)? • Does the PSHE curriculum celebrate diversity and explore the similarities of people?
Pupil involvement	• Does the school council regularly discuss the issue of bullying? • Do all pupils show an understanding of what bullying is, that it is unacceptable and what can be done about it? • Are pupils consulted about bullying issues?
Intervention	• Do all staff look out for signs of bullying? • Does the school have clear procedures for reporting bullying? • Are all pupils, parents/carers and school staff aware of these procedures? • Does the school have a 'culture of telling' when it comes to bullying? • Are all incidents of bullying dealt with with equal seriousness by all staff? • Are sanctions applied to bullies and is support offered to targets of bullying? • Are all bullying incidents followed up to check that it has not recurred? • Are the lines of communication in dealing with bullying consistent and clear? • Is the procedure for parental involvement in the intervention of bullying incidents clear and consistent? • Are children who bully or are likely to bully given opportunities to learn better ways of interacting with others? • Are children who are targets of bullying or likely to be targets of bullying given appropriate support?

CONTINUED

Issue	Points for consideration
Training	• Have school staff been given relevant training in positive behaviour and anti-bullying?
Environment	• Has the school investigated and addressed the increased likelihood of bullying in certain environments or at certain times of day in school? • Are pupils sufficiently supervised throughout the school day?
To and from school	• Has the school investigated any bullying off the school premises? • Is the school working in partnership with any taxi or bus services used to transport children to and from school? • Are there any other agencies that could be involved in ensuring pupils' safety beyond the school gates? (e.g. school traffic control officers)

• Develop relationships with school nurses, other health professionals, educational psychologists, mental health professionals, any available counselling services and social work resources that are or can be linked to your school. Make sure that teachers, counsellors, club leaders and other adults in the school know how to refer a pupil to available and relevant resources.

• Ensure that pupils learn 'cooling down' techniques throughout their school experience. Don't make it a one-time thing. Include the training in an array of subjects. Draw from established, tested curricula (e.g. SEAL) whenever possible.

9. CHILDREN AT RISK CAN BE HELPED

Effective schools recognise the potential in every student to overcome difficult experiences and to control negative emotions. Adults in these school communities use their knowledge of early warning signs to address problems before they escalate into physical or emotional bullying. These warning signs (which may be exhibited by bullies or their targets) include:*

• *Social withdrawal.* In some situations, gradual and eventually complete withdrawal from social contacts can be an important indicator of a troubled child. The withdrawal often stems from feelings of depression, rejection, persecution, unworthiness, and lack of confidence.

• *Excessive feelings of isolation and being alone.* Research has shown that the majority of children who are isolated and appear to be friendless are not violent. In fact, these feelings are sometimes characteristic of children and young people who may be troubled, withdrawn, or have internal issues that hinder development of social affiliations. However, research has also shown that in some cases feelings of isolation and not having friends are associated with children who behave aggressively and violently.

• *Being a target of violence.* Children who are targets of violence – including physical or sexual abuse – in the community, at school or at home are sometimes at risk of becoming violent towards themselves or others.

• *Feelings of being picked on and persecuted.* The young person who feels constantly picked on, teased, bullied, singled out for ridicule and humiliated at home or at school may initially withdraw socially. If not given

---

* (SOURCE: *Early Warning, Timely Response* by K. Dwyer, D. Osher and C. Warger (Washington, DC: US Department of Education, 1998)

adequate support in addressing these feelings, some children may vent them in inappropriate ways – including possible aggression or violence.

- *Excessive feelings of rejection.* In the process of growing up and in the course of adolescent development, many young people experience emotionally painful rejection. Children who are troubled are often isolated from their mentally healthy peers. Their responses to rejection will depend on many background factors. Without support, they may be at risk of expressing their emotional distress in negative ways – including violence. Some aggressive children who are rejected by non-aggressive peers seek out aggressive friends who, in turn, reinforce their violent tendencies.

- *Low school interest and poor academic performance.* Poor school achievement can be the result of many factors. It is important to consider whether a drastic change in performance and/or poor performance becomes a chronic condition that limits the child's capacity to learn. In some situations – such as when the low achiever feels frustrated, unworthy, chastised and denigrated – acting out and aggressive behaviours may occur. It is important to determine the emotional and cognitive reasons for the academic performance change to understand the true nature of the problem.

- *Expression of violence in writings and drawings.* Children and young people often express themselves in their drawings and in stories, poetry and other written expressive forms. Many children produce work about violent themes that for the most part is harmless when taken in context. However, an over-representation of violence in writings and drawings that is directed at specific individuals (family members, peers, other adults) consistently over time may signal emotional problems and the potential for violence. Because there is a real danger in misdiagnosing such a sign, it is important to seek the guidance of a qualified professional – such as a behavioural psychologist, counsellor or other mental health specialist – to determine its meaning.

- *Uncontrolled anger.* Everyone gets angry; anger is a natural emotion. However, anger that is expressed frequently and intensely in response to minor irritants may signal potential violent behaviour.

- *Patterns of impulsive and chronic hitting, intimidating and bullying behaviours.* Children often engage in acts of shoving and mild aggression. However, some mildly aggressive behaviours such as constant hitting and bullying of others that occur early in children's lives, if left unattended, may later escalate into more serious behaviours.

- *History of discipline problems.* Chronic behaviour and disciplinary problems both in school and at home may suggest that underlying emotional needs are not being met. These unmet needs may be shown in acting out and aggressive behaviours. These problems may set the stage for the child to violate norms and rules, defy authority, disengage from school and engage in aggressive behaviours with other children and adults.

- *History of violent and aggressive behaviour.* Unless provided with support and counselling, a young person who has a history of aggressive or violent behaviour is likely to repeat those behaviours. Aggressive and violent acts may be directed towards other individuals, be expressed in cruelty to animals or include arson. Young people who show an early pattern of antisocial behaviour frequently and across multiple settings are particularly at risk for future aggressive and antisocial behaviour. Similarly, young people who engage in overt behaviours such as bullying, generalised aggression and defiance, and covert behaviours such as stealing, vandalism, lying, cheating and arson are also at risk for more serious aggressive behaviour. Research suggests that age of onset may be a key factor in interpreting early warning signs. For example, children who engage in aggression and drug abuse at an early age (before age 12) are more likely to show violence later on than are children who begin such behaviour at an older age. In the presence of such signs it is important to review the child's history with behavioural experts and seek parents' observations and insights.

- *Intolerance for differences and prejudicial attitudes.* All children have likes and dislikes. However, an intense prejudice towards others based on race, ethnicity, sexual orientation, religion, social circumstances, gender, ability, disability and physical appearance, when coupled with other factors, may lead to violent assaults against those who are perceived to be different. Membership in hate groups or the willingness to victimise individuals with disabilities or health problems should also be treated as early warning signs.

- *Drug and alcohol use.* Apart from being unhealthy behaviours, drug and alcohol use reduce self-control and expose children and young people to violence, either as perpetrators, as targets, or both.

- *Affiliation with gangs or a peer group that exhibits negative and violent behaviours.* Peers who support antisocial values and behaviours – including extortion, intimidation, and acts of violence towards other pupils – cause fear and stress among other pupils. Young people who are influenced by these groups – those who emulate and copy their behaviour, as well as those who become affiliated with them – may adopt these values and act in violent or aggressive ways in certain situations. Gang-related violence and turf battles are common occurrences tied to the use of drugs that can result in injury and/or, in the worst cases, death.

- *Serious threats of violence.* Idle threats are a common response to frustration. Alternatively, one of the most reliable indicators that a young person is likely to commit a dangerous act toward self or others is a detailed and specific threat to use violence. Recent incidents across the country clearly indicate that threats to commit violence against oneself or others should be taken very seriously. Steps must be taken to under-

stand the nature of these threats and to prevent them from being carried out.

When warning signs indicate that danger is imminent, safety must always be the first and foremost consideration. Take action immediately. Emergency intervention by school authorities and possibly police officers is needed when a child:

- has presented a detailed plan (time, place, method) to harm or kill others – particularly if the child has a history of aggression or has attempted to carry out threats in the past

- is carrying a weapon, and has threatened to use it.*

In situations where students present other threatening behaviours, parents should be informed of the concerns immediately. School communities also have the responsibility to seek assistance from appropriate agencies, such as child and family services and community mental health services. These responses should reflect school policies and be consistent with the anti-bullying policy.

Effective school communities support staff, pupils and families in understanding the early warning signs. Support strategies include having:

- school policies in place that support training and ongoing consultation. The school staff know how to identify early warning signs, and understand the principles that support them

- school leaders who encourage others to raise concerns about observed early warning signs and to report all observations of imminent warning signs immediately. This is in addition to school policies that sanction and promote the identification of early warning signs

- awareness of any available specialists or trained staff who are identified as appropriate support for children with early warning signs.

---

* SOURCE: *Early Warning, Timely Response* by K. Dwyer, D. Osher and C. Warger (Washington, DC: US Department of Education, 1998).

It is recommended that each school develop clear referral systems for children with persistent behaviour problems or who exhibit early warning signs (e.g. to an educational psychologist or pastoral care worker). For example, in many schools the headteacher is identified as the first point of contact. If there is no immediate danger, the headteacher follows the usual procedures that are in place. If the concern is determined to be serious – but poses no immediate danger – it would be a good idea to involve the child's parents/carers.

The family should be consulted before implementing any interventions with the child. In cases where school-based factors are determined to be causing or worsening the child's troubling behaviour, the school should act quickly to modify them.

10. SCHOOLS ARE RESPONSIBLE FOR PROTECTING STUDENTS

Children cannot learn effectively if they fear for their safety. Troubled young people – both bullies and targets – need a supportive environment to learn and grow. In the words of Dr Dan Olweus, "Every individual should have the right to be spared oppression and repeated, intentional humiliation, in school and in society at large."

The DCSF document, 'Safe to Learn: Embedding anti-bullying work in schools' (00656–2007) clearly outlines the legal obligations of governing bodies, headteachers and teachers towards anti-bullying practice, promoting the well-being of individual pupils and safeguarding children. Furthermore, every school's Self-Evaluation Form needs to demonstrate that the school's planning is in line with the Every Child Matters agenda, which anti-bullying certainly contributes to.

Every school must now have a behaviour policy that explicitly outlines the measures that are taken in preventing all forms of bullying among pupils. Many schools choose to include these measures in a separate anti-bullying policy because of the profile this serious issue has in their school.

 Go further:
There are many legislative and guidance documents and websites that can be found on the Internet. These are a good source of keeping up-to-date with developments. Some that you might wish to access are listed in the back of this book.

'Bully' label
The term 'bully' is used throughout this book. The label is not intended to typecast pupils who bully others as 'bad people'. It is instead meant to refer to pupils when they are exhibiting bullying behaviours. Bullying is learned and can be unlearned. The goal is not to label or humiliate students who bully; rather, it is to help them stop using bullying behaviours. Recognising and treating a pupil as a person – one capable of showing positive actions – can help you do this. When talking with and helping pupils who bully others, do not use the label. Instead, focus attention on the inappropriate behaviour. Examples for doing this can be found on page 127.

Creating a
positive classroom

The tips and strategies in this section will help you create a classroom environment where everyone feels safe, accepted and appreciated. In a positive classroom, pupils can learn, teachers can teach, and education – not behaviour – is the focus.

These tips and strategies benefit everyone. Here are some good things you can expect to happen along the way:

Your pupils will learn how to:

- think and talk positively about themselves and others

- notice similarities and appreciate differences

- work together

- treat each other with kindness and respect

- give each other support and encouragement

- respond to bullying in ways that work

- resolve conflicts appropriately and effectively

- build empathy and realise that other people have feelings, wants and needs that are just as real and valid as their own.

You'll discover how to:

- clearly communicate a zero tolerance policy for bullying in your classroom

- reinforce your pupils' positive behaviours

- get to know and understand your pupils even better

- treat your pupils with greater kindness and respect

- model accepting, appropriate behaviour in all kinds of situations

- teach your pupils skills that will help them resolve conflicts, affirm themselves and each other, manage anger, make friends and be more assertive.

EXPOSE THE MYTHS

There are many myths about bullying. The 'True or False?' handout (page 19) will expose some of the myths and start students thinking about what bullying is and how it affects everyone. Answers with brief explanations are given on page 20.

You might read the answers aloud, and/or have pupils come up with their own reasons why each statement is a myth. Allow time for discussion. Make copies of the answers to give to pupils during or after the discussion.

DEFINE BULLYING

Before you can solve (or prevent) a problem, you first have to define it. If you and your pupils did the 'Expose the Myths' activity (above), everyone should have a general idea of what bullying *isn't*. (It isn't "just teasing", "normal", a "boy thing" etc.) You also want your pupils to agree on what it *is*. The process of defining it will help you arrive at a shared understanding and common language about bullying.

You might do this as a class, or divide the class into small groups and give them 10 minutes to work on a definition. Each group can choose one person to write down the group's ideas, and another to read the group's definition aloud when the class reconvenes.

Write pupils' definitions on the board. Then work together to come up with a class definition of bullying. Here are some concepts you can introduce into the discussion to keep pupils on track:

- Bullying takes at least two people: the bully and the target.

- Bullies like to feel strong and superior.

- Bullies enjoy having power over others.

- Bullies use their power to hurt other people.

Your class definition might use different words but should include these basic ideas:

- Bullying is being nasty to or hurting someone on purpose, repeatedly, over a period of time. Usually the people who are being bullied feel that they cannot stick up for themselves.

You might write the definition on the board and leave it there indefinitely or you could write it on a large piece of paper and display it prominently somewhere in the classroom.

BUILD ACCEPTANCE

When pupils accept each other, they are less likely to bully each other and more likely to defend targets of bullying. Here are three ways you can build acceptance in your classroom.

ACCEPTANCE STATEMENTS
Work with your class to come up with a list of 'acceptance statements' everyone (or most) can agree on. (Example: "We are all unique. Our differences make us interesting.") Have pupils make posters, collages, bulletin boards or displays illustrating the statements.

ACCEPTANCE PROJECTS
Explore fully the idea of acceptance. What does it mean and what is a person like if they are fully accepting (e.g. friendly, non-discriminatory, non-judgmental, happy to be with anyone...etc.)? Then brainstorm ways that would make people more accepting of each other (not judging, making the effort to be friendly to everyone, celebrating the fact that no two people are the same, remembering that everyone has feelings and likes to be treated well...etc.). Next explain to pupils that they are going to develop a campaign that has the sole purpose of making people more accepting of each other. What message needs to be put across to do this? Leave pupils to decide upon the method they are going to use to get their message across, e.g. a song, a TV advert, proverbs, a story, a poem, a poster, an article.

Let your pupils make the important decisions about what types of project to do. Be available to offer support and advice (and to suggest alternatives to projects that are clearly inappropriate), but try to let your pupils go wherever their creativity takes them. They might work individually or in small groups.

When the projects are finished, show them off at an assembly or Parents' Night. Invite family members, other teachers, and members of the community and the media to see what your pupils have accomplished and how they feel about acceptance.

"OUR CLASSROOM IS A PLACE WHERE . . ."

Distribute copies of the handout 'Our Classroom Is a Place Where . . .' (page 22) and discuss each statement. If pupils agree with the statements, they can sign and date their handouts. Post them around the room to show that your classroom is a place where people accept each other.

 Go further:
Send copies of the handout home so pupils can share them with their families.

When it's time to take down the handouts display, make a poster-sized copy of the original handout, hang it on a wall in your classroom, and leave it there. Refer to it often throughout the year. Discuss it with your pupils, with parents and caregivers at conferences, and with visitors to your classroom.

TALK ABOUT BULLYING

Have a class discussion about bullying. You might use the questions that follow. *But first*: tell pupils not to name names or point fingers. This should be a *general* discussion, not a time for blaming or accusing.

1. Who can tell me what bullying is?

   If you and your students did the 'Define Bullying' activity (page 17), someone can read the class definition.

2. What happens to people who are bullied? How do you think they feel?

3. How do you think bullies feel?

4. What happens to people who are around bullies and targets? What's it like to see someone get bullied? How does that make you feel?

5. Is there anyone who thinks bullying is a problem in our school? What makes you think that?

6. Is there anyone who thinks bullying is a problem in our classroom? What makes you think that?

7. Who would like to have an anti-bullying classroom?

8. What would it take to make our classroom an anti-bullying one? Who has ideas for doing this?

 Go further:
Write pupils' ideas on the board. Then have them vote for the top five. Try their ideas for a week or two. Let pupils assess their own progress towards making your classroom anti-bullying.

SHARE FACTS ABOUT BULLYING

If bullying is a problem in your school, you're not alone. Share and discuss these facts with your pupils:*

- About *one in seven* schoolchildren is either a bully or a target. (To illustrate this, you might have your pupils count off in sevens. Every seventh pupil can come to the front of the room or stay standing.)

- The helpline Childline took more than 30,000 calls on bullying last year – a quarter of its total.

- Ten to fifteen per cent of *all* children report being bullied on a regular basis.

- Bullying is more than beating people up. There are three basic types of bullying: physical, verbal and emotional. Most bullying is verbal.

* SOURCES: National Association of School Psychologists (NASP); *Education Week*; National Crime Prevention Council.

BULLYING: TRUE OR FALSE?

1. Bullying is just teasing.   T   F

2. Some people deserve to be bullied.   T   F

3. Only boys are bullies.   T   F

4. People who complain about bullies are babies.   T   F

5. Bullying is a normal part of growing up.   T   F

6. Bullies will go away if you ignore them.   T   F

7. All bullies have low self-esteem.
    That's why they pick on other people.   T   F

8. It's telling tales to tell an adult when you're
    being bullied.   T   F

9. The best way to deal with a bully
    is by fighting or trying to get even.   T   F

10. People who are bullied might hurt for a while,
    but they'll get over it.   T   F

1. **Bullying is just teasing.** **FALSE**

   Bullying is much more than teasing. While many bullies tease, others use violence, intimidation, and other tactics. Sometimes teasing can be fun; bullying *always* hurts.

2. **Some people deserve to be bullied.** **FALSE**

   No one ever deserves to be bullied. No one 'asks for it'. Most bullies tease people who are 'different' in some way. Being different is not a reason to be bullied.

3. **Only boys are bullies.** **FALSE**

   It seems that *most* bullies are boys, but girls can be bullies, too.

4. **People who complain about bullies are babies.** **FALSE**

   People who complain about bullies are standing up for their right not to be bullied. They're more grown-up than the bullies are.

5. **Bullying is a normal part of growing up.** **FALSE**

   Getting teased, picked on, pushed around, threatened, harassed, insulted, hurt and abused is *not* normal. Plus if you *think* it's normal, you're less likely to say or do anything about it, which gives bullies the green light to keep bullying.

6. **Bullies will go away if you ignore them.** **TRUE** and **FALSE**

   Some bullies might go away. But others will get angry and keep bullying until they get a reaction. That's what they want.

7. **All bullies have low self-esteem. That's why they pick on other people.** **FALSE**

   Some bullies have *high* self-esteem. They feel good about themselves, and picking on other people makes them feel even better. Most of the time, bullying isn't about high or low self-esteem. It's about having power over other people.

8. **It's telling tales to tell an adult when you're being bullied.** **FALSE**

   It's smart to tell an adult who can help you do something about the bullying. It's also smart to tell an adult if you see someone else being bullied.

9. **The best way to deal with a bully is by fighting or trying to get even.** **FALSE**

   If you fight with a bully, you might get hurt (and hurt someone else). Plus you might get into trouble for fighting. If you try to get even, you're acting the same as the bully. And the bully might come after you again to get even with *you*. Either way only makes things worse.

10. **People who are bullied might hurt for a while, but they'll get over it.** **FALSE**

    Bullying hurts for a long time. Some children do not do well at school because of bullying. Some became so sad, desperate, afraid and hopeless that they committed suicide. Many adults can remember times when they were bullied as children. People don't 'get over' being bullied.

- Most bullying happens at school where there is little or no supervision. *Examples*: in the playground, in the corridors, in the dining hall and toilets.

- Bullying hurts everyone. *Targets* feel sad, afraid, anxious, and bad about themselves. They may have social problems (a hard time making friends), emotional problems (low self-esteem, loneliness) and academic problems (their schoolwork suffers). *Witnesses* (people who see or hear others being bullied) may feel afraid and anxious. *Bullies* often get into serious trouble as adults; statistics show that one in four bullies will have a criminal record before the age of 30, and many have problems with relationships throughout their lives.

Go further:
Have pupils do library or Internet research about bullying and gather facts of their own. They might report their facts orally or in writing. Or create a 'Bully Facts' bulletin board.

NAME BULLYING BEHAVIOURS

What do bullies do? Your pupils – whether targets or bullies – probably know the answer(s) to this question. Ask them and list their responses on the board. Your list might include several (or all) of the following. If your pupils focus mostly on physical bullying (hitting, kicking etc.), introduce some of the other behaviours listed here (act rude, embarrass people, ignore people etc.). Pupils need to understand that bullying encompasses a broad spectrum of behaviours, none of which are 'normal' or acceptable.

- act like they rule the world
- act mean
- act rude
- attack people
- boss people around
- brag about being tough
- break people's things

- carry weapons or things they intend to use as weapons
- cheat
- damage people's things
- embarrass people
- force people to hand over their money
- force people to hand over their possessions
- frighten people
- gossip
- harass people
- hit
- humiliate people
- hurt people's feelings
- ignore people
- insult people
- intimidate people
- kick
- laugh at people
- leave people out
- lie
- make fun of people
- make obscene gestures
- make racist, homophobic or sexist comments
- make people feel helpless
- make people feel inferior
- make people feel invisible
- make people do things they don't want to do
- make people feel uncomfortable
- name-call
- pick on or attack people because of their race, religion, gender, family background, culture etc.
- pick on or attack people because they're different in some way
- push
- put people down
- refuse to talk to people
- reject people
- say nasty things about people
- say sarcastic things to people

We don't all have to be the same.

We don't all have to think the same.

We don't all have to act the same.

We don't all have to talk the same.

We don't all have to dress exactly the same.

We don't all have to believe the same things.

We have the right to be ourselves.

We like it that people are different.

We know that our differences
make us interesting and UNIQUE.

We honour different ways of being, acting,
and believing – even when we don't agree with them.

We do our best to solve problems peacefully.

**We speak up if we see others being treated
unfairly.**

*We treat each other the way we'd
like to be treated.*

We treat each other with respect.

- scare people
- scream
- send threatening or insulting texts
- shove
- spread rumours
- steal
- swear
- take people's things
- taunt
- tease
- tell mean jokes
- threaten
- touch people in rude or abusive ways
- use chat rooms or websites to humiliate
- use physical violence
- use verbal taunts
- write nasty things about people
- yell

 Go further:
Turn the list into a class promise. Provide an extra-large piece of paper, markers, magazines (for cutting out pictures), tape, glue, scissors etc. Write across the top in big letters: 'As a class, we promise NOT to. . . .' Then let pupils add words, phrases, illustrations, pictures, etc. to create a colourful poster for your classroom wall – or the corridor outside your classroom. They can all sign their names across the bottom.

TACKLE CYBERBULLYING

As a relatively new form of bullying, cyberbullying needs to be fully acknowledged and understood so that it is readily recognised as bullying. Cyberbullying is quite simply, using technology (e.g. mobile phones, e-mails, chat rooms, video hosting sites, social network sites etc) to pass on information, images and messages that upset another person.

All bullying is serious, but cyberbullying can be particularly impactful on account of the speed at which information can be shared, and because this kind of bullying can happen at any time of the day, night and week.

To consider cyberbullying, pupils can look at the sheet *Cyberbullying – the key issues* on page 25.

 Go further:
Detailed guidance and a summary leaflet can be found by typing 'cyberbullying' into the search box at: http://publications.teachernet.gov.uk

TACKLE HOMOPHOBIC BULLYING

Homophobic bullying and homophobic language occur in many primary schools. Children with gay parents/carers or relatives, those who do not fall in line with gender stereotypes and children who are or are perceived to be different in some way can all experience homophobic bullying. Homophobic language can be aimed at any child or adult as an insult in schools where homophobia has not been addressed.

Homophobic bullying includes insults, cyberbullying, ostracising and any other forms of bullying. The main difference between homophobic bullying and other types is that targets are less likely to report homophobic bullying because they feel embarrassed or do not want to disclose their sexuality.

If homophobia is challenged consistently at primary school, foundations will be laid for more beneficial attitudes towards same-sex couples, resulting in less homophobic bullying at secondary school. It is important that the whole school community understands why homophobia needs to be challenged.

Here are key points to help staff consider this issue.

- Nearly all primary schools will have pupils who will grow up to be gay.

- Many people consider gay and lesbian relationships to be about love and respect in the same way that heterosexual relationships can be.

- Some individuals in some religions have strong views about lesbian and gay relationships. All faiths, however, clearly take the view that any kind of bullying is wrong.

- At primary school, challenging homophobia is as much about school ethos as the curriculum. A school ethos that celebrates diversity of every kind and aims to prevent anyone being picked on for real or perceived differences is valuable. The curriculum needs to reflect the positive school ethos and to be inclusive. This means that resources and lessons should represent people from the full spectrum of diversity and not promote any one type of relationship as 'normal'.

- Some children use the word 'gay' to be rude to another person. This is not acceptable – even if the person does not know what the word means. It is using a word that is used to describe a group of people as an insult. If a child used a strong racist term, we would challenge it whether or not they knew what it meant. Using the word gay as an insult can be challenged simply by saying, 'Gay means when two men or two women love each other; it is not acceptable to use that word as an insult.'

- Homophobic bullying causes a lot of suffering. Suicide rates for gay men are significantly higher than for straight men.

 Go further:
Detailed guidance can be found by typing 'homophobic bullying' into the search box at: http://publications.teachernet.gov.uk

SHARE STORIES ABOUT BULLYING

Distribute copies of the handout 'Bullying Stories' (page 27). Tell your pupils that they will use the handouts to write about their own experiences with bullying – as someone who was bullied; as someone who bullied another person; as someone who witnessed a bullying incident and did nothing about it; and as someone who witnessed a bullying incident and either got help or tried to stop it.

Call attention to the 'No Names Rule' at the top of the handout. If some pupils don't understand how they can tell their stories without using names, give examples. ("Someone called me a bad name." "I knocked someone's books off his desk on purpose." "I saw one person trip another, but I didn't say anything." "I told someone to stop pushing my friend.")

Divide the class into small groups (no more than five pupils each).

 Important:
If you're aware that one pupil in your classroom has been bullying another, make sure those two pupils aren't in the same group.

Allow quiet time for pupils to write their stories. Then allow time for them to share their stories within their groups. Reconvene the class and ask a spokesperson from each group to briefly summarise the stories.

Have a class discussion about the stories. You might ask questions like these:

- Did we hear stories about people getting bullied? How did those stories make you feel?

- Did we hear stories about people bullying others? How did those stories make you feel?

- If you saw or heard someone being bullied, what would you do?

- Did we hear good ways to stop bullying or get help? Are there any ideas you might try if you see or hear someone being bullied in the future?

You might end by saying, "To all of you who saw or heard bullying and did something about it – congratulations! You're Bully Busters!"

What is cyberbullying?

Cyberbullying is the use of technology (e.g. mobile phones and the Internet) to send images or messages that upset someone.

1. **Some cyberbullying is accidental**

   A person can send a message or an image that is forwarded on to more people. This can cause a lot of upset. Think carefully before you send any message using the Internet or a mobile phone. You might not mean to offend anyone, but if what you send causes upset it can be difficult to undo the damage – text and pictures can stay in 'cyberspace' for a long time.

2. **Don't share your personal details (or anyone else's)**

   Keep passwords private. Only give your mobile phone number and email address to trusted friends. Never hand another person's contact details over to someone without their permission.

3. **Never reply or retaliate**

   This will never help to sort out the cyberbullying.

4. **Save all evidence**

   Keep phone numbers, e-mail addresses and any messages that offend you as these are evidence of the cyberbullying and will make it easier to deal with.

5. **Never suffer in silence – always report cyberbullying**

   ...to someone you trust

   This might be your parent/carer or another adult you trust. If the adult you tell does nothing to help, then find another to tell. Keep telling until someone helps.

   ChildLine (0800 1111) is a free helpline for children and young people. Advisors are available at any time of the day or night to give advice about any problem you might be having.

   ...to the service provider

   Many websites have a way of blocking messages if you report cyberbullying to them. Mobile phone companies can block particular numbers.

   ...to your school

   Schools have a responsibility to deal with any bullying that happens to one of their pupils. This includes bullying, such as cyberbullying, that happens outside the school grounds.

6. **Find out more:**

   Many websites offer advice on dealing with cyberbullying. Here are three:

   Directgov – http://yp.direct.gov.uk/cyberbullying/

   Kidscape – http://www.kidscape.org.uk/childrenteens/cyberbullying.shtml

   Stop Cyberbullying – http://www.stopcyberbullying.org/index2.html

How much bullying goes on in your classroom, and what kinds? You've probably noticed specific instances, and pupils might have told you about others. But most bullying goes *unnoticed* and *unreported*.

It goes unnoticed because:

- Bullies tend to hurt or abuse others when adults aren't around to see it.

- Bullies act in ways that adults aren't aware of or don't notice.

It goes unreported because:

- Targets are ashamed of being bullied, afraid of retaliation, or worried that adults can't or won't help them.

- Bystanders – or witnesses – don't want to get involved, or they don't interpret what they're seeing as bullying, but as 'teasing' or 'normal' or 'children being children' behaviour.

If you want to know what's happening in your classroom, ask your pupils. One of the best, simplest, least intimidating ways to do this is by taking a survey.

You might use one or both of the surveys on pages 28–32. Or invite your pupils, their parents, and other teachers and staff to help you create a survey. If your school or local authority is using a bully prevention programme, a survey instrument might already exist.

The primary purpose of the surveys on pages 28–32 is to gather information about the types of experience your pupils are having, not to point fingers at specific individuals. If you want a survey to help you identify pupils who are being bullied, have pupils write their names on it. Otherwise, keep it anonymous. When you ask pupils to sign their names, some might be reluctant to admit to certain items. Anonymity might lead to more honest responses.

Depending on your pupils' age(s) and reading level(s), you might want to read a survey aloud.

Some pupils might need individual assistance completing the survey.

Give each pupil as much privacy as possible when completing a survey. Tell pupils that the survey isn't a test (they won't be marked), but it's like a test in two important ways: No looking at anyone else's survey. No talking during the survey.

ABOUT 'THIS WEEK IN SCHOOL' (pages 28–29)

This survey describes things that might happen to a pupil during a typical week. About half of the things described are pleasant or neutral; about half are unpleasant. This keeps the focus on pupils' experiences in general, not just bullying.

Introduce the survey with a brief explanation. *Example*:

> "This checklist lists things that might or might not happen to you in school. Like: 'This week in school, another pupil in my class called me names.' Or: 'This week in school, another pupil in my class said something nice to me.' Read each statement and think about the past week. How often did this happen to you? Never? Once? More than once? Answer by putting a tick in that column."

Since the survey asks about "this week", it's best to give it on a Friday. If your pupils are very young, you might want to ask them what happened to them yesterday or even today; their memories of an entire week might be sketchy or inaccurate.

Use the survey as it is or adapt it to meet the needs of your pupils. If you adapt it, make sure to include a balance of positive, neutral, and negative items. Also make sure you include these six key statements:

4. tried to kick me
8. said they'd beat me up
10. tried to make me give them money
23. tried to hurt me
36. tried to break something of mine
38. tried to hit me

BULLYING STORIES

Use the spaces below to write about experiences from your life.
NO NAMES RULE: Don't use anybody's name.

Describe a time when someone's words or behaviour hurt you.	Describe a time when you said or did something to hurt another person.
Describe a time when you saw/heard bullying but didn't do anything about it.	Describe a time when you saw/heard bullying and either got help or tried to stop it.

Over to you

THIS WEEK IN SCHOOL

Read each statement and think about the past week. Put a tick in
the column that describes how often that happened to you during the week.
When you're finished with the checklist, give it to the teacher.

Today's date:_____

Tick this box if you're a boy ☐   Tick this box if you're a girl ☐

This week in school, another pupil in my class:	Never	Once	More than once
1. called me names			
2. said something nice to me			
3. said something rude or mean about my family			
4. tried to kick me			
5. treated me with kindness and respect			
6. was mean to me because I'm different			
7. gave me a present			
8. said they'd beat me up			
9. gave me some money			
10. tried to make me give them money			
11. tried to scare me			
12. loaned me something I wanted to borrow			
13. stopped me from playing a game			
14. was mean about something I did			
15. talked about clothes with me			
16. told me a joke			
17. told me a lie			
18. got other people to gang up on me			

CONTINUED

THIS WEEK IN SCHOOL (CONTINUED)

This week in school, another pupil in my class:	Never	Once	More than once
19. tried to make me hurt someone else			
20. smiled at me			
21. tried to get me in trouble			
22. helped me carry something			
23. tried to hurt me			
24. helped me with my schoolwork			
25. made me do something I didn't want to do			
26. talked about TV with me			
27. took something away from me			
28. shared something with me			
29. said something rude or mean about the colour of my skin			
30. shouted at me			
31. played a game with me			
32. tried to trip me			
33. talked with me about things I like			
34. laughed at me in a way that hurt my feelings			
35. said they would tell on me			
36. tried to break something of mine			
37. told a lie about me			
38. tried to hit me			
39. made me feel bad about myself			
40. made me feel good about myself			

BULLYING SURVEY

Read each question and answer it as honestly as you can.
Think about this definition of bullying as you answer the questions:

BULLYING IS WHEN A STRONGER, MORE POWERFUL PERSON HURTS OR FRIGHTENS A SMALLER OR WEAKER PERSON DELIBERATELY (ON PURPOSE) AND REPEATEDLY (AGAIN AND AGAIN).

Today's date: _____

Your name (if you want to give it): _____

Tick this box if you're a boy ☐   Tick this box if you're a girl ☐

1. Is anyone mean to you when you're in our classroom? yes ☐   no ☐
   If *yes*, what do they do to you? _____
   _____
   _____

   How often does this happen? (Once a day? Twice a day? Several times a day? Once a week? Once a month?) Your answer:
   _____

2. Is anyone mean to you at breaktime?   yes ☐   no ☐
   If *yes*, what do they do to you? _____
   _____
   _____

   How often? _____

3. Is anyone mean to you at lunch?   yes ☐   no ☐
   If *yes*, what do they do to you? _____
   _____
   _____

   How often? _____

➡️ *CONTINUED*

4. Is anyone mean to you in the toilets?   yes ☐   no ☐
   If *yes*, what do they do to you? _____
   _____
   _____
   How often? _____

5. Is anyone mean to you in the corridors?   yes ☐   no ☐
   If *yes*, what do they do to you? _____
   _____
   _____
   How often? _____

6. Without naming the bully (or bullies), describe him or her by ticking statements in this list:
   The bully is . . .
   ☐ about my age   ☐ younger than me   ☐ a girl
   ☐ older than me   ☐ a boy   ☐ a whole group
   ☐ what else? _____

7. Have you ever told anyone at school that you're being bullied?   yes ☐   no ☐
   If *no*, why don't you tell someone? _____
   _____
   If *yes*, who did you tell? _____
   _____
   What did the person do to help you? _____
   _____
   After you told, did the bullying stop?   yes ☐   no ☐
   After you told, did the bullying get worse?   yes ☐   no ☐

CONTINUED →

8. How has the bullying affected you? Has it changed your life in any way? Think about how you feel (good? okay? bad? sick? scared?); how you feel about yourself; how you're doing in school; who your friends are; and anything else you think might relate to being bullied.

_____

_____

_____

9. How long have you been bullied? (A week or less? Two or three weeks? A month? A few months? Half a year? A year? More than a year? A few years? Many years? Your whole life?) Your answer:

_____

10. Have you ever bullied someone else?   yes ☐   no ☐

    If *yes*, what did you do?_____

    _____

    Why did you do it? _____

    _____

    How did it make you feel?_____

    _____

11. Are you bullying anyone now?   yes ☐   no ☐

    If *yes*, would you like to stop?   yes ☐   no ☐

12. What can we do to stop or prevent bullying in our classroom?

    _____

    _____

    _____

    _____

    _____

For these six statements:

- Add up the number of times a tick was placed under "more than once". Do this separately for each statement. (*Example*: For "4. tried to kick me", three pupils said "more than once".)

- Divide the score for each statement by the number of surveys completed to get the percentage of pupil responses. (*Example*: 3 pupils divided by 25 in the class = 12%.)

- Add all six percentages. (*Example*: 12 + 8 + 12 + 20 + 5 + 10 = 67%.)

- Divide this number by 6. (*Example*: 67 divided by 6 = 11.16%.)

This gives you an idea of how many pupils in your classroom are being bullied or are at risk of being bullied.

You can do the same maths for ticks placed under "once" for the six key statements. This gives you an idea of the level of aggression in your classroom.

ABOUT THE 'BULLYING SURVEY'
(pages 30–32)

You might give this survey to the whole class, use it to interview individual pupils you suspect of being bullied, or use it to interview small groups of pupils to get a feeling for what types of bullying and how much goes on in your classroom.

Introduce the survey with a brief explanation. *Example*:

> "Bullying is being nasty to or hurting someone on purpose, repeatedly, over a period of time. Usually the person who is being bullied feels that they cannot stick up for themselves. Often, pupils who are bullied don't tell other people about it. They feel bad inside, or they're afraid that the bully might get back at them for telling, or they're worried that no one will help them if they tell.

> "Everyone has a right not to be bullied. No one deserves to be bullied. This survey is a safe way to tell me if you're being bullied at school. You don't have to give anyone's name. You don't even have to sign it unless you want to. If you do sign it, I'll arrange to talk with you in private. So you can answer the questions honestly."

Use this survey as it is or adapt it to meet the needs of your pupils. For example, you might want to:

- limit it to questions about bullying in your classroom (skipping those about break-times, lunch, the toilets and the corridors)

- expand it with questions about bullying on the way to and from school (at the bus stop, on the bus, while walking or biking etc.), at school-sponsored events (sporting events, assemblies, fairs, concerts, club meetings etc.) and elsewhere in the school building or on the grounds (in the changing room, between buildings, in the gym etc.)

- add questions about specific types of bullying (teasing, name-calling, pushing, shoving, hitting, kicking, shouting, tripping, intimidating, ignoring, rejecting, threatening, taking possessions, excluding, swearing, spreading rumours, lying, harassing etc.)

- gather additional demographic information (race, ethnic background, religion etc.) to try to determine whether bullies are targeting a particular group of pupils.

SET RULES

Establish and enforce class rules about bullying and behaviour. Rules clearly communicate a zero tolerance for bullying and an expectation of positive behaviour. They also meet pupils' physical and psychological needs for safety; it's hard to learn when you're intimidated, threatened and scared, or when you're a witness to intimidating, threatening and scary behaviour.

For rules to be effective, they should be:

- created with pupil input

- short and simple

- easy to understand

- specific

- agreed upon and accepted by everyone

- enforceable

- enforced consistently and fairly

- communicated to and supported by parents, other teachers and staff

- reviewed periodically and updated when needed.

Note: If your school or local authority has already established rules about bullying and behaviour, share these with your pupils. If the language seems too complicated, have pupils put the rules in their own words.

If you're free to make your own class rules, get everyone involved. Have a class discussion or break up into small groups. Ask pupils to come up with answers to these questions:

- What kind of classroom do you want to have?

- What can everyone do to make this happen?

When pupils set their own rules (instead of being told to follow rules imposed by adults), they learn to manage their own behaviours. Work together to come up with a list of rules; depending on the age of your pupils, you might limit the total number to five or ten (the fewer the better). Examples are provided in the box.

You might write the rules on a poster headed 'Our Class Rules' and have everyone sign their names.

What will be the consequences of breaking the rules, and how can you enforce them? This might depend on existing school rules. Or work with your class to determine fair and reasonable consequences.

Post the rules in your classroom where everyone can see them. For a time, you might start each day by reading the rules aloud (or having a pupil read

1. **Bullying is not allowed in our classroom.**

2. **We don't tease, call people names or put people down.**

3. **We don't hit, shove, kick or punch.**

4. **If we see someone being bullied, we speak up and stop it (if we can) or go for help straight away.**

5. **When we do things as a group, we make sure that everyone is included and no one is left out.**

6. **We make new pupils feel welcome.**

7. **We listen to each other's opinions.**

8. **We treat each other with kindness and respect.**

9. **We respect each other's property. (School property, too.)**

10. **We look for the good in others and value differences.**

them). Once you feel confident that your pupils know the rules – and you've seen evidence that they're following them – you can read them weekly. Every month or so, review the rules with your class to see whether any changes are needed. Don't hesitate to revise the rules. Tell your class that the rules aren't written in stone and there's always room for improvement.

 Go further:
Communicate the rules and consequences to parents in a letter home, and share them with other teachers and staff.

DESIGNATE YOUR CLASSROOM ANTI-BULLYING

If you and your pupils did the 'Talk About Bullying' activity (page 18), chances are they all agreed that they would like to have an anti-bullying classroom (question 7).

Ask whether they're willing to designate their classroom anti-bullying – a place where people accept each other, value each other and treat each other with kindness and respect. If they are, brainstorm ways to formalise and publicise your class commitment. *Examples*:

1. Make a poster or banner announcing "This Is an Anti-Bullying Classroom." Display it in the corridor outside the classroom.

2. If your class publishes a newsletter or newspaper, devote an issue to the topic of what it means to be an anti-bullying classroom. Invite pupils to write articles, draw cartoons, do interviews etc.

3. Write a press release announcing that your classroom has decided to be anti-bullying. Send it to your local media (newspapers, magazines, radio stations, TV stations). They might follow up with a story about your pupils.

 Go further:
Have pupils visit other classrooms and encourage them to become anti-bullying. They can also meet with the headteacher, explain what your class is doing, and ask him or her to announce that your whole school is committed to being anti-bullying.

TEACH ANGER MANAGEMENT SKILLS

What happens to most of us when we're in danger or under stress? We experience the 'fight-or-flight' response. We battle the cause of the danger we perceive or the stress we experience... or we run as fast as we can to get away.

When pupils are bullied, running away is an option; sometimes it's the only option. Your pupils need to know that fighting is not an option, except in cases where self-defence is essential.

What can they do instead of fighting or trying to hurt someone back? They can learn and practise other ways to manage their anger.

Distribute copies of the handout '20 Things to Do Instead of Hurting Someone Back' (page 38) and go over it with the pupils. Explain that this handout gives them 20 *different* ways to manage their anger. Ask whether they know other ways that work, and list them on the board.

 Go further:
The British Association of Anger Management (BAAM) offers bespoke anger management programmes to children, teachers and parents. You can contact them on 0845 1300 286 or email info@angermanage.co.uk. On the web go to www.angermanage.co.uk

ENCOURAGE PUPILS TO REPORT BULLYING AND RESPOND EFFECTIVELY

Much (even most) bullying occurs where adults can't see it and intervene. Bullies don't want adult audiences. You need to rely on pupils for information about bullying you don't witness personally. How can you encourage them to come forward? You might want to post these suggestions in your classroom:

- If you *see* someone being bullied, tell the teacher.

- If you *know* that someone is being bullied, tell the teacher.

- If you *think* that someone might be bullied, tell the teacher.

- If you *do nothing* about bullying, you're saying that bullying is okay with you.

- We have the power to stop and prevent bullying in our classroom, but we have to work together!

If everyone in a school feels responsible for anti-bullying action, its pupils will be more likely to report bullying incidents. This will be true not only of children that are being bullied but also of those that have witnessed bullying. Witnesses need to be aware of their role and responsibilities 1) as not becoming an audience that provides the bully with approval for their actions, 2) as someone who could report the bullying and 3) as someone who could support the person who has been bullied and persuade them to report the incident themselves. It is important, however, to make it clear that witnesses should never put themselves at risk of harm.

How each individual responds to seeing someone being bullied depends on: whether they feel safe, whether they feel like they could influence the bully or the audience and whether they feel they know an adult whom they can tell about bullying and who will take suitable action.

How can pupils tell you about bullying? Give them several options. If they're comfortable doing this, they can tell you face-to-face – before or after school, in private (especially if they fear reprisals from the bully). Or they can write about bullying in their diaries (see 'Weekly Diary', pages 42–43). Or they can write you a note (see 'Use a Notes-to-the-Teacher Box', pages 45 and 46).

The photocopiable sheet Develop a Culture of Telling – Witnesses to Bullying on page 37 can be used to explore what pupils should do if they witness bullying.

No matter how much you encourage your pupils to keep you informed about bullying in your classroom, *reporting will stop* if you don't respond quickly and effectively. Your pupils need to trust that if they risk telling you about bullying, you'll do something about it. Anything less compromises or destroys that trust.

Your school or local authority might already have procedures in place for intervening with bullying and responding to reports of bullying. If so, follow these procedures. You'll find additional tips and suggestions in the 'Helping Targets' and 'Helping Bullies' sections of this book.

INTERVENE IMMEDIATELY WHEN YOU WITNESS BULLYING

You're the teacher. It's your classroom – and your responsibility to intervene immediately with any bullying you witness, whether it's physical (pushing, shoving, hitting, tripping), verbal (teasing, name-calling, racist or bigoted remarks) or emotional (intimidating, ignoring, excluding). When you intervene effectively, you accomplish four important goals:

1. You put a stop to that particular bullying incident.

2. You make it clear that you won't tolerate bullying in your classroom.

3. You show that you're an adult who will do something about bullying, not just ignore it.

4. Your behaviour encourages other targets and witnesses to tell you about bullying you don't witness personally.

You'll find intervention tips and strategies in the 'Helping Targets' and 'Helping Bullies' sections of this book.

TEACH FRIENDSHIP SKILLS

Some children become bullies because they don't have friends, feel lonely, and seek attention by bullying. Some children become targets because they're isolated and easier to pick on. All pupils – bullies, targets and everyone else – can benefit from learning and practising friendship skills. Here are two activities you can try with your pupils.

Anti-bullying is everyone's responsibility. We are more likely to combat bullying if everybody is prepared to report it when it happens.

This is what some pupils said when they were asked:

What would you do if you saw someone being bullied?

- I think I would just ignore it and walk away – that would be the best thing to do.

- I wouldn't put myself in danger by tackling the bully, but I think I would have to go and tell an adult about what I had seen.

- I think that bullies like it when people watch them – so I would walk on – and definitely not watch.

- If you see someone being bullied, you could make the bully know that you think what they are doing is wrong. If there were lots of people around, you could try and persuade people to stop the bullying. I think most people know bullying is wrong and would want it to stop.

- I think you should join in with the bully so they don't pick on you too.

- I think it is down to the person who has been bullied to go and tell an adult about what has happened.

- I think you should support the person who has been bullied – after the bullying has stopped.

1. Which of these answers do you agree with?

2. If you saw bullying, what would you do?

3. Write a set of guidelines for people who witness bullying.

20 THINGS TO DO INSTEAD OF HURTING SOMEONE BACK

When someone hurts you, it's normal to feel angry. You might even want to get back at the person by hurting him or her. But you can choose not to do that. You can do one (or more) of these things instead.

1. STOP and THINK. Don't do anything right away. Consider your options. Think about what might happen if you try to hurt the other person.

2. Know that what you do is up to you. You can decide. You are in charge of your actions.

3. Tell yourself, "It's okay to feel angry. It's not okay to hurt someone else. Even if that person hurt me first."

4. Tell the person, "Stop that! I don't like that!"

5. Keep your hands to yourself. Make fists and put them in your pockets.

6. Keep your feet to yourself. Jump or dance or stomp.

7. Walk away or run away.

8. Tell the person how you feel. Use an 'I message'. *Example*: 'I feel angry when you hit me because it hurts. I want you to stop hitting me.'

9. Take a deep breath, then blow it out. Blow your angry feelings out of your body.

10. Find an adult. Tell the adult what happened and how you feel.

11. Count slowly from 1 to 10. Count backwards from 10 to 1. Keep counting until you feel your anger getting smaller.

12. Think cool thoughts. Imagine that you're sitting on an iceberg. Cool down your hot, angry feelings.

13. Think happy thoughts. Think of something you like to do. Imagine yourself doing it.

14. Treat the other person with kindness and respect. It won't be easy, but give it a try. This will totally surprise the other person, and it might end the conflict between you.

15. Draw an angry picture.

16. Sing an angry song. Or sing any song extra loud.

17. Remember that getting back at someone never makes conflict better. It only makes it worse.

18. Take a time-out. Go somewhere until you feel better.

19. Find another person to be with.

20. Know that you can do it. You can choose not to hurt someone else. It's up to you.

FRIENDSHIP TIPS

Distribute copies of the handout '12 Tips for Making and Keeping Friends' (page 40). Read and discuss each tip in turn and check for understanding. During the discussion, you might ask pupils to give examples from their own experience of how they have used these friendship skills. You might also comment on times when you've seen pupils use these skills with each other.

 Go further:
Challenge your pupils to choose one friendship tip to work on during the next week. Then, at the end of a week's time, ask them to report on their progress. They might do this orally or in writing.

FRIENDSHIP BOOSTERS AND BUSTERS

Ask your pupils, "What makes someone a good friend?" Invite them to think about their own friends and what they like most about them. Write their ideas on the board under the heading 'Friendship Boosters'. *Examples:*

- **A good friend is always there for you.**

- **A good friend is someone who listens.**

- **A good friend is someone who likes you for who you are.**

- **A good friend is someone you can trust.**

- **A good friend is someone who trusts you.**

- **A good friend is honest.**

- **A good friend encourages you to do and be your best.**

- **A good friend is someone who understands you.**

- **A good friend is someone who shares with you.**

- **A good friend respects your property.**

- **A good friend respects your rights.**

- **A good friend is fair.**

- **A good friend is someone who sticks up for you.**

- **A good friend doesn't try to get you to do things you shouldn't do.**

Next, ask your pupils, "What kinds of thing can hurt a friendship or keep people from making friends?" Write their ideas on the board under the heading "Friendship Busters". *Examples:*

- bragging
- name-calling
- being bossy
- teasing
- making fun of others
- being stuck-up
- lying
- spreading rumours
- stealing
- being rude
- being sarcastic
- ignoring people
- making people feel left out
- cheating
- hitting
- being mean
- embarrassing people
- trying to get people to do things they don't want to do or shouldn't do.

If you and your pupils did the 'Name Bullying Behaviours' activity (pages 21 and 23), someone will probably notice the similarities between these 'Friendship Busters' and bullying behaviours. If not, point it out. You might ask questions like these:

12 TIPS FOR MAKING AND KEEPING FRIENDS

1. **Reach out.** Don't always wait for someone else to make the first move. A simple hi and a smile go a long way.

2. **Get involved.** Join clubs that interest you. Take special classes inside or outside of school. Be a volunteer.

3. **Let people know that you're interested in them.** Don't just talk about yourself; ask questions about them.

4. **Be a good listener.** Look at people while they're talking to you. Pay attention to what they say.

5. **Risk telling people about yourself.** When it feels right, let them in on your interests, your talents, and what's important to you.

BUT . . .

6. **Don't be a show-off.** Not everyone you meet will have your abilities and interests. (On the other hand, you shouldn't have to hide them – which you won't, once you find friends who like and appreciate you.)

7. **Be honest.** Tell the truth about yourself, what you believe in, and what you stand for. When asked for your opinion, be sincere. Friends appreciate truthfulness in each other. BUT . . .

8. **Be kind.** There are times when being tactful is more important than being totally honest. The truth doesn't have to hurt.

9. **Don't just use your friends as sounding boards for your problems.** Include them in the good times, too.

10. **Do your share of the work.** That's right, *work*. Any relationship takes effort. Don't always depend on your friends to make all the plans.

11. **Be accepting.** Not all of your friends have to think and act like you do. (Wouldn't it be boring if they did?)

12. **Learn to recognise the so-called friends you can do without.** Some people get so lonely that they put up with anyone – including friends who aren't really friends at all.

- Can acting like a bully ruin a friendship?

- Can acting like a bully get in the way of making friends?

New pupils are more likely to be accepted if they join your class at the start of the school year. If a new pupil arrives during the year, make a special effort to welcome him or her.

A day or two before the new pupil is due to arrive, alert your class. If you have any information about the new pupil (has the family recently moved from another town, city or county? does the pupil have any special talents, interests, abilities or needs?), share it with the class. Ask questions like these:

- How would you feel if you were new in our school? If you were new in our class?

- How would you want us to treat you?

- What would make you glad to be in our class?

- What can we do to make (pupil's name) feel welcome?

Brainstorm ideas with your class. Here are a few starter ideas:

- Create a colourful "Welcome (Pupil's Name)!" banner to hang in your room.

- Make greetings cards to give the new pupil.

- For the first week or two, ask for volunteers to be the new pupil's 'buddy' – showing him or her around, making introductions, sitting with him or her at lunch etc. *Tip*: Change buddies every day or every other day. Make sure that buddies come from different groups within the class.

- Create a 'Welcome Pack' to give to the new pupil. You could include a school handbook (either one made by other pupils or anything the school already has), term dates, a timetable, a map of the school, a list of all the people in the class with some details

about each of them, some welcome messages from each member of the class, information about school clubs, a special treat of some kind (written promises of kindness from other pupils, a sticker, a badge, a pencil top) and anything else you or your pupils can think of that might be useful or fun.

CREATE A CLASS BOOK

Invite each pupil to write a one-paragraph description of himself or herself. Pupils might include their likes, dislikes, talents, interests, club memberships, goals, hopes for the future, or anything else they'd like other people to know about them. You could invite pupils to fill up two sides of A4 paper about themselves in a magazine-style format.

When all the pupils have completed their sheets, bind them together to make a class book. Have the book available for pupils to look at during reading sessions or registration. These books are usually very popular and help pupils get to know more about each other.

EXPLORE EXPECTATIONS

Sometimes other people behave in ways in which we expect them to behave. We communicate our expectations – in words, actions and body language – and other people respond in kind. Similarly, how we treat others is often based on our expectations. Does this mean that changing our expectations can change someone else's behaviour – or our own behaviour? It's worth exploring.

As a class, talk about the power of expectations. You might ask questions like these:

- Where do our expectations of people come from? Our own experiences? Things other people have told us? Or a combination of the two?

- Do you think expectations can influence our behaviour? Why or why not?

- If you expect someone to treat you with kindness and respect, how do you act towards that person?

- If you expect someone to be mean or rude to you, how do you act towards that person?

- If someone has high or positive expectations of you, how do you know? How does that make you feel?

- If someone has low or negative expectations of you, how do you know? How does that make you feel?

- Do you think that changing your expectations of another person might change the way you treat him or her?

- Do you think that changing your expectations of another person might change the way he or she treats you?

You might illustrate these concepts with examples from your own experiences. Or use examples like these:

- "[Pupil's name], imagine that each day when you come to class, I expect you to interrupt me, tease people sitting near you and refuse to do your schoolwork. How will I treat you? How will you act then?"

- "[Pupil's name], imagine that each day when you come to class, I expect you to be polite, helpful and ready to work. How will I treat you? How will you act then?"

- Imagine if a new pupil was about to join the class. How would you react to them if (a) you had been told that they were a really lovely person or (b) you had heard that they were really mean and nasty – before you had even met them? How would it affect how you greeted them?

Suggest that pupils try this activity:

1. Think of someone you don't usually get along with. How do you expect him or her to treat you? How do you communicate your expectations?

2. Try changing your expectations for a few days or a week. See whether that makes a difference in how the person treats you – and how you treat him or her.

If your pupils are keeping diaries (see the next activity), you might ask them to record their thoughts and experiences.

Summarise by asking the class:

- What might happen if we all came to school each day expecting the *worst* from each other? How would we treat each other? How would we act? What kind of classroom would we have?

- What might happen if we all came to school each day expecting the *best* from each other? How would we treat each other? How would we act? What kind of classroom would we have?

- What if we all expected our classroom to be anti-bullying every day? Would we work to make it that way? To keep it that way?

LEARN MORE ABOUT YOUR PUPILS

The more you know about your pupils, the better you can meet their learning needs – and their needs to belong, feel accepted and get along with each other. This all contributes to a positive classroom environment.

You're probably doing many things already to know your pupils better: greeting them by name when they enter your classroom, communicating with them one-on-one, asking about their days and weeks, listening when they come to you with a problem, concern or exciting news. Here are two more ideas you may want to try.

WEEKLY DIARY
Reading your pupils' diary entries can give you insight into their actions and help you understand the problems they face each day. Commenting on their entries – with brief, encouraging notes, never

criticisms – can strengthen your relationship and improve two-way communication.

If possible, provide your pupils with notebooks. Then introduce the activity by saying something like this:

> "Each week, I'll give you a topic to write about in your diary. I'll ask you to write about your thoughts or feelings, something you care about or something important to you. Your entries can be as long or as short as you want, but I'd like you to write at least a paragraph. I'll collect the diaries and keep them between diary times. I'll be reading your diaries as a way to get to know you better. I'll also be writing back to you with my own thoughts and responses. Your diaries will never be marked or criticised. Think of this as another way for us to communicate with each other."

Here's a short list of sample topics to start with. Create your own topics based on what you learn about your pupils and what you'd like to know.

- a time when I felt happy
- a time when I felt sad
- a time when I felt proud
- a time when I felt scared
- the last time I helped someone
- the last time I got into trouble
- my definition of a friend
- my definition of caring
- my greatest achievement
- my hopes for the future.

Consider keeping your own diary and sharing your entries with your class as you see fit.

MY FAVOURITE THINGS
Distribute copies of the handout 'My Favourite Things' (page 44). When pupils complete them, you can either collect the handouts to review privately,

invite pupils to tell the class about some of their favourite things, or post the handouts around the room and give pupils time to read them. *Tip*: Tell your pupils ahead of time which option you'll choose, in case they prefer to keep their responses private.

If the handouts are shared, you might have a class discussion about them. Ask questions like these:

- Did you discover that you have things in common? What things?
- Were there any surprises?
- Did you learn anything new? What did you learn?
- Are there things that everyone likes?
- Are there things that no one likes?

 Go further:
Have pupils create a poster or bulletin board listing and/or illustrating things they have in common.

IDENTIFY ROLE MODELS

Who are your pupils' role models? Celebrities? Family members? Other adults they know and admire? Friends? This is an excellent topic for a class discussion – and it reveals a great deal about who your pupils look up to and are likely to want to emulate.

When more than 1000 young people ages 13–17 were asked, "If you could pick one person to be your role model, which of the following categories would your role model be in?" the box on page 45 shows how they responded.*

Ask your pupils to name their role models. So they don't all 'follow the leader' and name the same person (or someone a friend names), have them write their role models' names on a piece of paper, sign them and give them to you. You might also ask them to list one or two reasons why they admire these people. Encourage them to think

---

* SOURCE: *The State of Our Nation's Youth 1998–1999* (Alexandria, VA: Horatio Alger Association of Distinguished Americans, Inc., 1998).

MY FAVOURITE THINGS

Today's date: _____

Your name: _____

My favourite TV programme	My favourite place to go	My favourite thing to do in my free time	The thing I like MOST about school	The thing I like LEAST about school
My favourite athlete/sports personality	My favourite radio station	My favourite food	My favourite place to eat	I like people who
I don't like it when people	My favourite magazine	My favourite book	My favourite film	My favourite website
The job I'd like to have when I grow up	My favourite game	My greatest hope	My biggest worry	If I could go anywhere in the world, I'd go to
My favourite type of music	My favourite singer/group/musician	My favourite actor/actress	The person I admire most	My favourite time of the day

Family members	40.7%
Friends/family friend	14.4%
Teaching/education	11.1%
Sports/sports-related	10.3%
Entertainment industry	4.9%
Religious leader	4.3%
Business leader	1.9%
National political leader	0.5%
International political leader	0.4%
Local political leader	0.0%
Other	11.6%

about people they know, not just the usual sports figures, actors, singers and other celebrities.

Set aside time to talk about role models. You might ask questions like these:

- What makes someone a role model?

- Why is it important to have role models?

- Why do you admire your role models? What special qualities do they have? Are these qualities you would like to have someday?

- Are your role models a positive influence on you? In what ways?

- Are your role models people who accept others? How can you tell?

You might also identify your own role models and tell your pupils why you admire them.

EXPLORE WAYS TO DEAL WITH BULLIES

What should you do when someone bullies you? Many pupils don't know the answer to that question. Of course, there isn't just one right answer; it depends on the specific situation. But certain responses are generally more effective than others.

The 'What Should You Do?' handout (page 47) invites pupils to consider several possible responses to bullying. Answers with brief explanations are given on pages 48–49.

You might read the answers aloud, and/or have pupils come up with their own reasons why each response would or wouldn't work. Allow time for discussion. Make copies of the answers to give to pupils during or after the discussion.

Note: Answers are presented as 'best answers' because each real-life situation is different. At the end of this activity and discussion, pupils should understand that: (1) there's more than one way to respond to bullying, (2) some responses can make things better, and (3) some responses can make things worse.

 Important:
Tell pupils that in some situations – when they're being bullied by a gang, when they're in real danger of getting beaten up or worse, when there's any chance that a weapon might be present – the best response is always to get away as fast as you can and tell an adult.

USE A NOTES-TO-THE-TEACHER BOX

Put a 'Notes-to-the-Teacher Box' on the corner of your desk. It might be large or small, decorated or plain. It should be lockable and have a lid with a slit in the top.

To explain the purpose of the box, you might say:

"Here's another way for you to communicate with me. If there's anything you want to tell me about – a problem you're having at school, a classroom issue, an exciting event, or anything at all you'd like me to know – just write me a note and drop it in the box. I'm the *only* person who can open the box and read the notes inside, and I'll check the messages at the end of each day.

"You don't have to sign your name if you don't want to, but I hope you will. I can only reply to you personally if you sign your name.

"You can also use the box to tell me about bullying in our classroom. You can write about bullying that happens to you, or bullying you witness personally. If you've been bullying someone else and you want to stop, you can write about that, too."

Then be sure to follow through. Check the box daily. Respond appropriately to the notes your pupils write. If pupils have special concerns, arrange to meet them privately.

If notes reveal that some of your pupils are being bullied or are bullying others, try the suggestions in the 'Helping Bullies' and 'Helping Targets' sections of this book.

 Important:
If a pupil uses the box to disclose abuse or another serious problem, you have a legal responsibility to help your pupil to get the support and assistance he or she needs.

PROMOTE STRUCTURED ACTIVITIES

Much bullying takes place during unstructured activities, especially breaktime. Encourage your pupils to plan ahead for those times and tell you their plans. What will they do during breaktime? Will they play a game? What kind of game? Who will play? What about the pupils who won't take part in the game – what will they do? If you're one of the playground supervisors, you can watch to make sure pupils follow through with their plans. If you're not, you can ask them to report back to you after breaktime. Try to get them in the habit of deciding in advance how they will spend unstructured time. If they have difficulty making plans, offer suggestions.

You might also explore the possibility of assigning older and younger children to different playground areas. Talk with the headteacher and other teachers; work out an arrangement together.

PROVIDE SUPERVISION

It's believed that some children become bullies because the supervision they get at home is minimal or non-existent. And bullies tend to do their bullying where adults can't observe and intervene. You can't supervise your pupils at home, but you can – and should – supervise them at school. This may be one of the most effective bully prevention strategies available to you.

1. Start by considering the level of supervision in your own classroom. Are you able to keep an eye on all (or most) of your pupils all (or most) of the time? If you're in charge of a large class, this may be difficult or impossible. How can you bring more adults into your classroom? Arrange for a student teacher or invite parent helpers into the class. Involving sixth-form pupils from a local secondary school in supporting your class on a voluntary basis might also be possible.

2. Are you aware of bullying problems on the playground, in the dining hall, and/or in the corridors? Get together with other teachers and teaching assistants and share what you've heard (or overheard). Increase the number of playground and dining hall supervisors. Since changing rooms are common places for bullying, teachers should keep an eye on changing rooms during class changes.

It's true that spending more time supervising pupils will increase your workload. But the results are worth it. More supervision equals fewer bullying incidents, especially serious incidents. More positive supervision – where you interact with pupils, suggest ways they can interact with each other, and model kindness, acceptance, affirmation and getting along – promotes more positive behaviour. Before long, everyone feels safer and more secure, the school climate noticeably improves – and you're spending *less* time dealing with bullying and behavioural problems.

What should you do when someone bullies you?
Read each idea and decide whether you think this is something you might do.
Tick 'Yes' if you would, 'No' if you wouldn't, or 'Not sure'.

When someone bullies you, you should:	Yes	No	Not sure
1. cry			
2. tell a friend			
3. tell the bully's parents			
4. run away			
5. try to get even with the bully			
6. tell a teacher			
7. stay home from school			
8. hit, push or kick the bully			
9. stand up straight, look the bully in the eye, and say in a firm, confident voice, "Leave me alone!"			
10. hunch over, hang your head, and try to look so small the bully will stop noticing you			
11. laugh and act like you just don't care			
12. stand up straight, look the bully in the eye, and say in a firm, confident voice, "Stop it! I don't like that."			
13. tell your parents/carers			
14. threaten the bully			
15. stay calm and walk away			
16. call the bully a bad name			
17. shout, "Cut it out!" as loudly as you can			
18. ignore the bully			
19. tell a joke or say something silly			
20. if other people are nearby, join them so you're not alone			

When someone bullies you, you should:

1. **cry**   Best answer: **NO.**

   Bullies love having power over others. They enjoy making people cry. When you cry, you give them what they want. On the other hand, you might be so upset that you can't help crying. If this happens, get away as quickly as you can. Find a friend or an adult who will listen and support you.

2. **tell a friend**   Best answer: **YES.**

   Make sure it's a friend who will listen, support you and stand up for you. And don't just tell a friend. Tell an adult, too.

3. **tell the bully's parents**   Best answer: **NO.**

   Some children become bullies because their parents bully them. The bully's parents are more likely to believe their child, not you. They might even get defensive and blame you.

4. **run away**   Best answer: **NOT SURE.**

   If you feel you're in real danger – for example, if you're facing a gang of bullies – then run as fast as you can to a safe place. At other times, it might be better to stand your ground and stick up for yourself. Follow your instincts!

5. **try to get even with the bully**   Best answer: **NO.**

   The bully might get angry and come after you again. Plus getting even means you are using bullying behaviour too.

6. **tell a teacher**   Best answer: **YES.**

   Especially if the bullying happens at school. Most bullying happens where adults aren't likely to see or hear it. Your teacher can't help you unless you tell (or someone else tells).

7. **stay home from school**   Best answer: **NO.**

   Unless you feel you're in real danger, you should never stay home from school to avoid a bully. Remember, bullies love power. Imagine how powerful they feel when they can scare someone away from school! Plus staying home from school gets in the way of your learning and hurts you even more.

8. **hit, push or kick the bully**   Best answer: **NO.**

   If you use violence, chances are you'll get hurt. Plus you might get in trouble for fighting.

9. **stand up straight, look the bully in the eye, and say**   Best answer: **YES.**
   in a firm, confident voice, "Leave me alone!"

   Bullies don't expect people to stand up to them. They usually pick on people who don't seem likely to defend themselves. So they're surprised when someone acts confident and strong instead of scared and weak. This might be enough to make them stop.

CONTINUED ➡

10. **hunch over, hang your head, and try to look so small the bully will stop noticing you**   Best answer: **NO.**

This gives bullies what they want – someone who appears even *more* scared and weak.

11. **laugh and act like you just don't care**   Best answer: **NOT SURE.**

Some bullies will give up if people don't react to their bullying. But others will bully harder to get the reaction they want.

12. **stand up straight, look the bully in the eye, and say in a firm, confident voice, "Stop it! I don't like that."**   Best answer: **YES.**

See number 9.

13. **tell your parents/carers**   Best answer: **YES.**

Tell them what's happening and ask for their help.

14. **threaten the bully**   Best answer: **NO.**

The bully might get angry and come after you even harder.

15. **stay calm and walk away**   Best answer: **YES.**

Especially if you can walk towards a crowded place or a group of your friends.

16. **call the bully a bad name**   Best answer: **NO.**

This will only make the bully angry – bad news for you.

17. **shout, "Cut it out!" as loudly as you can**   Best answer: **YES.**

This may surprise the bully and give you a chance to get away. Plus, if other people hear you, they might turn and look, giving the bully an audience he or she doesn't want.

18. **ignore the bully**   Best answer: **NO.**

Bullies want a reaction from the people they're bullying. Ignoring them might lead to more and worse bullying.

19. **tell a joke or say something silly**   Best answer: **NOT SURE.**

Sometimes humour can defuse a tense situation. Be careful not to tell a joke *about* the bully or make fun of him or her.

20. **if other people are nearby, join them so you're not alone**   Best answer: **YES.**

Bullies generally don't pick on people in groups. They don't like being outnumbered.

BUILD EMPATHY

Empathy is the ability to identify with and understand another person's feelings, situation, motives and concerns – to put ourselves in someone else's place or, as the saying goes, "in someone else's shoes". This is one of the most important traits we develop – and the sooner the better.

Empathy is basic to positive relationships with friends, peers, family members and everyone else we encounter throughout our lives. Often, when children aren't liked by others, it's because they lack empathy. Research has shown that children are born with a predisposition towards empathy. However, if it isn't encouraged and supported, it doesn't grow.

It's not enough for pupils to empathise with people they have things in common with. That's easy. They also need to empathise with people who are very different from them – in their needs, experiences, points of view, life circumstances, beliefs, ethnic and cultural backgrounds, talents, abilities, accomplishments etc. They need to be able to think about how other people feel – and, eventually, how other people *might* feel or *would* feel in response to specific events and circumstances.

There are many ways you can build empathy in your pupils. Here are four ideas you can try.*

ASK QUESTIONS
During lessons, group work and other times, ask questions that draw pupils' attention away from themselves and towards the feelings, needs and concerns of others. *Examples*:

How would you feel if . . .

- you were the new child in school?

- you were the most popular pupil? the least popular pupil?

- someone made fun of you or called you names?

- you came to school every day without eating breakfast?

- your parents were divorced?

- someone picked on you all the time?

- you didn't have a home or a safe place to live?

- walking down the street was dangerous?

- you were the smallest child in class?

- you were the biggest child in class?

- you couldn't speak English very well?

- you found reading difficult?

- you used a wheelchair?

- you wore glasses?

- you couldn't hear well or at all?

- you had an illness and felt sick a lot of the time?

These and other questions might be topics for class discussions or diary writing (see 'Weekly Diary', pages 42–43).

 Go further:
The SEAL curriculum includes many visual aids showing a variety of emotions and circumstances. Use pictures that show a variety of emotions and situations and ask pupils to describe how they think the person is feeling and why. This helps to develop empathy and emotional literacy.

TAKE OUT-OF-SCHOOL TRIPS
Expose pupils to people whose lives are different from their own. You might visit a children's home, a homeless shelter, a children's hospital, a senior citizens' home. When appropriate, you and your pupils might build relationships (with frequent visits) or start a pen-pal exchange. Or you might volunteer as a class to help at one of the places you visit. Plan volunteer experiences carefully. Check with your headteacher about procedures, and be sure to get permission from pupils' parents.

---

* See also 'Build Understanding', pages 62–63.

LEAD AN IMAGINATION EXERCISE

Have pupils sit comfortably and quietly in their chairs (or on the floor – you'll need cushions or a rug) with their eyes closed. Ask them to imagine that another person is sitting directly across from them. This should be someone they don't know very well, or someone they have neutral or negative feelings about. Then guide them with questions and suggestions like these:

- Picture the person in your mind. Is it a man or a woman? A boy or a girl? What colour hair does the person have? What colour eyes? What is he or she wearing? How is he or she looking at you?

- Say to yourself, "[The person's name] is a human being. So am I. This is something we have in common."

- Ask yourself [pause between each question to allow time for pupils to think about it]:

  - What do I really know about this person? Where does my knowledge come from? My own experience with him or her? Things other people have said? Rumours? Gossip? My own prejudices or biases?

  - What might be important to this person?

  - What is something this person might like? What is something this person might not like?

  - What are this person's needs? What does he or she want out of life?

  - What are some reasons this person acts the way he or she does?

  - What problems might this person have?

  - What might this person find difficult?

  - What might this person be afraid of?

  - What might this person wish he or she could do?

End by asking, "Were you able to see the world through the other person's eyes? How did that feel? What did you discover about the person – and about yourself?"

HELP STUDENTS DEVELOP A FEELINGS VOCABULARY

It's easier to empathise with feelings we can name. There are many ways you can help your pupils develop a feelings vocabulary. Here are some starter ideas:

- Invite pupils to name their feelings. When they enter your room, say, "Hello, [name]! How are you feeling today?"

- Make a large 'pockets poster' for your room. Tape or staple several pockets to a piece of posterboard. Label each pocket with a feeling. (*Examples*: happy, sad, excited, worried, tired, wide awake, confused, anxious, contented.) Cut strips of paper (or construction paper) and write one pupil's name on each strip. When pupils arrive in your classroom, each puts his or her name strip in the pocket that best describes how he or she is feeling. (This also gives you a general idea of the 'mood' your class is in.)

- Use books, videos and posters to explore feelings and ways to express them.

- Play a "What Am I Feeling?" game. Pair pupils and have them sit across from each other. As one pupil imagines feeling a certain way and shows it in his or her body language and facial expression, the other pupil tries to identify and name the feeling.

- Distribute copies of the handout '50 Words That Describe Feelings' (page 52). Practise the words with your pupiils. Make sure they understand what each one means. Invite them to use the words in class discussions, in written work and reports. You might also include them in spelling lessons.

50 WORDS THAT DESCRIBE FEELINGS

happy
excited
eager
joyful
'on top of the
world'

shy
bashful
helpless
lonely
unsure

sad
'down'
gloomy
miserable
tearful

confused
puzzled
mixed-up
distracted
tired

fidgety
anxious
tense
worried
restless

irritated
mad
angry
upset
furious

calm
content
satisfied
proud
relaxed

fearful
embarrassed
guilty
self-conscious
ashamed

surprised
startled
afraid
shocked
terrified

safe
secure
confident
hopeful
trusting

REWARD COOPERATION

Often, when we plan group activities for our pupils, we focus on the *product* – the paper, project or other end result we expect them to accomplish. Another equally important (more important?) aspect of group activities is teaching pupils how to cooperate as they work towards a common goal.

Plan some group activities that stress this as the main purpose. *Examples*:

- a craft project designed so each pupil can make a contribution

- an anti-bullying classroom campaign, complete with posters, slogans, songs and short plays

- friendship role-plays

- kind-word crosswords or wordsearch puzzles

- new games for the rest of the class to play.

Emphasise the value of effort over results. Establish checkpoints along the way during which pupils can report on how well they're working together, whether they're enjoying the process, and what they're learning from each other.

Sit in with each group, observe, and comment on what you see. Compliment pupils for their willingness to get along and value each other's unique abilities.

This type of group activity offers several rewards. It encourages unity and acceptance and discourages perfectionism. It invites pupils to take risks and explore new interests without fear of rejection. It gives them opportunities to acquire new skills and reveal hidden strengths, which boosts their standing among their peers. When pupils cooperate, everybody wins.

KEEP MARKS PRIVATE

Most pupils are concerned about the marks they get for their work. Those that do really well or fall behind are at increased risk of being bullied. For this reason (among others), you should keep marks and test scores private.

- If your pupils mark their own papers, collect them afterwards and record the scores yourself. Don't ask them to call out their results.

- If you have pupils mark each other's homework assignments and quizzes, reconsider this practice. It probably saves you time, but is it good for your pupils? Have you noticed any who seem embarrassed or uncomfortable when their papers are being marked by their classmates? Have you noticed pupils making fun of someone else's papers? Even if you haven't witnessed these behaviours personally, it doesn't mean they're not happening.

- Never discuss a pupil's marks where other pupils might overhear.

- Don't display high or low test scores in your classroom. Celebrate pupils' achievements in other ways.

USE QUOTATIONS AS TEACHING TOOLS

Collect quotations about friendship, peace, peacemaking, self-esteem, assertiveness, tolerance, understanding, acceptance, kindness, respect and other topics related to creating a positive classroom. Invite your pupils to bring in quotations they find.

Begin each day with a positive quotation, then ask your pupils to offer their thoughts on what it means – and what it means to them personally. Ask them to keep the quotation in mind throughout the day. *Tip*: Quotations also make good diary writing assignments. (See 'Weekly Diary', pages 42–43.)

Here are several quotations you may want to use to start your collection:

- "If you judge people, you have no time to love them." *Mother Teresa*

- "A friend is a present you give yourself." *Robert Louis Stevenson*

- "Maturity begins to grow when you can sense your concern for others outweighing your concern for yourself." *John MacNaughton*

- "What we see depends mainly on what we look for." *John Lubbock*

- "Change your thoughts and you change your world." *Norman Vincent Peale*

- "We each need to do what we can to help one another no matter how tiny it is. If we do something for peace – each of us – we can all make the difference." *Mairead Corrigan Maguire (1976 Nobel Peace Prize Winner)*

- "Friendship is the only cement that will ever hold the world together." *Woodrow Wilson*

- "It is not enough simply to 'live and let live': genuine tolerance requires an active effort to try to understand the point of view of others." *Aung San Suu Kyi (1991 Nobel Peace Prize Winner)*

- "Blessed are we who can laugh at ourselves, for we shall never cease to be amused." *Anonymous*

- "Never be bullied into silence. Never allow yourself to be made a target. Accept no one's definition of your life, but define yourself." *Harvey Fierstein*

- "Friendship with oneself is all-important, because without it one cannot be friends with anyone else." *Eleanor Roosevelt*

Random acts of kindness are proven, powerful ways to create a more positive environment anywhere – in the classroom, at home and in the community. Here are five activities you can do with your pupils to promote kindness and help them form the habit of doing nice things for others "just because".

CLASS DISCUSSION

Talk about kindness as a class. You might ask questions like these:

- When was the last time someone did something really nice for you? What did the person do? How did it make you feel?

- Did the person have a reason for acting that way? Did he or she expect something from you in return? Or was the person kind "just because"?

- Have you ever done something nice for another person without being asked, and without expecting anything in return? What did you do? How did you feel? How do you think the other person felt?

- What if everyone in this class made the effort to be kind to each other? What would our class be like? Is this something we should try? How can we start?

Ask pupils to offer suggestions. List them on the board. Have them vote on one or more to try for the rest of the week.

 Go further:
Read from the book *Kids' Random Acts of Kindness* (D. Markova, Conari Press, 1994) or from *Random Acts of Kindness* (D. Wallace, Ebury Press, 2004). Use the ideas in the book to discuss how acts of kindness can make you feel – whether you do them or have them done to you. Pupils could try and think up some random acts of kindness that they could do around school.

KINDNESS BOX

Take a box with a lid (a large shoebox works well) and cut a slit in the top. Decorate it (or have pupils decorate it). Label it the 'Kindness Box' and put it on a shelf or a corner of your desk.

Invite pupils to write brief notes about acts of kindness they do or witness and drop them in the box. Once a week, once a day, or whenever you choose, dip into the box, pull out a note and read it aloud to the class. Thank your pupils for their kindness to each other.

KINDNESS PALS

Write your pupils' names on slips of paper, put the slips in a hat or box and have pupils draw names. (Anyone who draws his or her own name should try again.) Explain that by the end of the week, everyone should do at least one act of kindness for the person whose name they drew. If you think your pupils might need ideas, brainstorm some as a class and write them on the board to serve as reminders.

At the end of the week, invite pupils to tell the class what they did. After each pupil reveals his or her act of kindness, lead the class in applause.

If your pupils are keeping diaries (see pages 42–43), you might ask them to write about their acts of kindness. When you read their entries, be sure to leave a positive comment or two congratulating them on their efforts.

KINDNESS REPORTER

Select one pupil each week to serve as a 'kindness reporter'. He or she will watch for acts of kindness and briefly describe them in a notebook. (*Tip*: Children might enjoy using a special notebook provided for this purpose.) At the end of the week, have the reporter share the good news with the class.

BIG BOOK OF KINDNESS

Ask your pupils to watch for and collect stories about kindness. They might write brief descriptions of stories they see on television or in films, or bring in stories from newspapers or magazines.

They might write stories about kindness they experience in their own lives – at home, at school, in their neighbourhoods, in clubs or organisations they belong to and so on.

As pupils gather their stories, have them paste or write them on large sheets of paper. They can decorate them with drawings, photos, collages or whatever they choose. Punch holes along the edges and bind the sheets together with pieces of string or yarn. Add cardboard covers with decorations and the title 'Our Big Book of Kindness'. Keep the book available so pupils can look through it and add to it often.

TEACH PUPILS TO USE 'I MESSAGES'

'I messages' are simple, powerful ways to communicate our wants, needs and feelings. When you teach your pupils how to use them, you're giving them a tool that will help them in many different situations – including times when they're confronted by a bully.

You might introduce 'I messages' by saying:

> "Sometimes we need to tell other people exactly how we feel and why. Maybe they're bothering us or bullying us and we want them to stop what they're doing and leave us alone.

> "An 'I message' is a good way to communicate what we want. When we use an 'I message', we say what we need without blaming the other person. Blaming can make a problem worse. It puts the other person on the defensive."

Distribute copies of the handout 'Five Steps to an "I Message"' (page 56) and go over the steps with the pupils. Invite them to give other examples of messages they might use. Have them create and perform brief role-plays showing 'I messages' in action.

FIVE STEPS TO AN 'I MESSAGE'

1. **Always start with 'I', not 'You'. 'I' puts the focus on your feelings, wants and needs. 'You' puts the other person on the defensive.**

   "I _____"

2. **Clearly and simply say HOW you feel.**

   "I feel _____"   *Example*: "I feel angry."

   "I'm _____"   *Example*: "I'm upset."

3. **Clearly and simply say WHAT the other person did (or is doing) that made you feel that way.**

   "I feel _____ when you _____"   *Example*: "I feel angry when you call me names."

   "I'm _____ because you _____"   *Example*: "I'm upset because you tripped me."

4. **Clearly and simply say WHY you feel the way you do.**

   "I feel _____ when you _____ *because* _____"

   Example: "I feel angry when you call me names. because I have a real name."

   "I'm _____ because you _____ and _____"

   Example: "I'm upset because you tripped me and I dropped my books all over the floor."

5. **Clearly and simply say WHAT you want or need the other person to do.**

   "I want you to _____"

   Example: "I feel angry when you call me names because I have a real name. I want you to start calling me by my real name."

   "I need you to _____"

   Example: "I'm upset because you tripped me and I dropped my books all over the floor. I need you to help me pick up my books."

HELP PUPILS TO UNDERSTAND PEER INFLUENCE

At the top end of primary school and at secondary school the significance and therefore influence of pupils' peers usually increases. This can be because pupils no longer have such a close relationship with a single teacher, and because of an increased need for independence from the adults in their lives – i.e. growing up.

Increased 'peer influence' can be a positive or a negative thing, depending on the peer group. Pupils sometimes find themselves 'going along' with things that they do not really want to do, to fit in with the majority.

Helping pupils to understand this effect can encourage them to consider their actions more carefully. Are they doing something because everyone else is doing it, or because they really want to do it?

The photocopiable sheet How Much do Your Peers Influence You? on page 58 can be used to guide discussions about peer influence.

TEACH ASSERTIVENESS SKILLS

Some pupils don't know what to do or how to react when they're bullied. Should they cry? Run away? Fight back? Get even? Do nothing? If your class did the 'Explore Ways to Deal with Bullies' activity (page 45), you've discussed some effective and ineffective ways to respond. On the 'What Should You Do?' handout (page 47), two of the ways listed (numbers 9 and 12) are *assertive* responses to bullying.

In general, bullies tend to be *aggressive* – they behave as if their rights matter more than anyone else's rights. Targets tend to be *passive* – they behave as if other people's rights matter more than theirs. *Assertive* people respect their own rights *and* other people's rights.

Most of us could benefit from assertiveness training. Here are some tips and strategies for teaching your pupils to be more assertive. Practise them with your pupils and offer coaching where needed. Pupils who are naturally shy and withdrawn, and those who have been (or are) bullying targets, will need extra help learning and using assertiveness skills.

KNOW YOUR RIGHTS
Ask your pupils, "Do you have any rights? Do you know what they are?" As they offer ideas, write them on the board. Make sure that these rights appear somewhere on the list below:

 Go further:
Have pupils create and illustrate a 'Pupil Bill of Rights' poster for the classroom.

1. **We have the right to think for ourselves.**

2. **We have the right to have and express our opinions, views and beliefs as long as they do not damage other people's rights.**

3. **We have the right to make decisions about our lives.**

4. **We have the right to say no.**

5. **We have the right to say yes.**

6. **We have the right to stand up to people who tease us, criticise us or put us down.**

7. **We have the right to have and express our feelings.**

8. **We have the right to respond when someone violates our rights.**

WATCH YOUR BODY LANGUAGE
Sometimes body language speaks more loudly than words. Children who slouch, mumble, fidget, avoid looking people in the eye, back off and appear frightened and worried are more likely to be targets than those whose body language expresses confidence and positive self-esteem.

Peers – people your own age or close to your age that you spend time with

Influence – the power something has over you.

THEREFORE

Peer Influence = the power your friends and acquaintances have over you.

Discuss these questions with a partner:

1. If all your friends started having their hair styled in a particular way, how important would it be for you to make yours match?

2. If someone laughed at your shoes, would you:

    a) stop wearing them

    b) keep wearing them but feel very self-conscious

    c) tell the person that you just have different tastes and that they should not be so rude and keep wearing them?

3. If a group of your friends were teasing and laughing at a person that you did not know, would you

    a) join in

    b) stay quiet, but watch

    c) tell your friends to stop?

4. Can you think of anything that you have done JUST because all your friends were doing it?

CONTINUED

5.   Can you think of anything that you do that is different from your friends? If so, what do your friends say about it?

Consider peer influence

If you place a lot of importance upon what your friends think of you, you will always be looking for their approval. This can mean you end up going along with whatever your friends are doing whether you really want to or not.

Here are some key points about peer influence:

- Being different sometimes takes courage.

- Being true to yourself can sometimes mean that you are not going along with the crowd.

- Many people admire someone who has the confidence to stick out from the crowd.

- Just because all your friends are doing something – doesn't mean it's always a great thing to do.

- Before doing anything it is a good idea to ask yourself whether you *really* want to do it or not.

- Your friends' views will understandably be important to you but if they are making you do something you are unhappy about, you have the right to challenge their views.

It's not right – those children don't *deserve* to be bullied any more than other children – but it's true.

Teach pupils how to look assertive. Practise with role-plays, play and face-to-face discussions. Here are the five basics of assertive body language:

1. Stand up straight. Stand with your feet slightly apart so you feel balanced and stable.

2. Keep your head up.

3. Keep your shoulders straight. Don't hunch.

4. Look people in the eye. Not over their heads, not at the ground – right in the eye.

5. Don't back off when you're talking to someone. Move closer – but not too close. Keep a comfortable distance between you.

When you *look* assertive, you're more likely to *feel* assertive. And other people are more likely to treat you with respect.

Pair assertive body language with assertive words, spoken in a firm, confident, determined voice. Don't mumble or whine – but don't shout, either. Then say what you mean and mean what you say. Use 'I messages'. (See page 55.)

USE THE ASSERT FORMULA

Distribute copies of the handout 'The ASSERT Formula' (page 61) and lead pupils through it. Have them practise the formula in short plays and role-plays.

 Go further:
There are many more resources that aim to develop children's assertiveness. There are also assertiveness training programmes available in some parts of the country. Kidscape run ZAP Assertiveness Training sessions. See www.kidscape.org.uk/zap for details.

PROMOTE TEAMWORK

Pupils who participate in group activities are more likely to have positive feelings about other people. They develop fewer biases and prejudices – or rethink the biases or prejudices they already have.

Talk as a class about the attitudes, skills and abilities people need to work well in groups. Ask your pupils to think about what makes a good team member and a good team. Write their ideas on the board. If they have difficulty coming up with ideas, you might start by offering one or more of these.

Good team members...

- accept each other as equals
- support the group's goals
- support the group's rules
- participate in discussions
- listen to each other during discussions
- disagree without being disagreeable
- express their needs and feelings honestly
- do their fair share of the work
- have a positive attitude
- suggest solutions to problems.

Good teams...

- set clear goals and agree to reach them together
- set clear rules and agree to follow them
- resolve any disagreements fairly and peacefully
- identify the strengths of individual team members, then use those strengths to benefit the team as a whole
- compromise when there's a conflict
- share the responsibilities equally among the team members.

You might ask your class:

- Do you think our class is a good team? Why or why not?
- What could we do to work better as a team? Who has specific ideas we can try?

A stands for **Attention**. Before you can talk about and try to solve a problem you're having with someone else, you need to get his or her attention. *Example*: "Sean, I need to talk to you about something. Is now a good time?"

S stands for **Soon, Simple, and Short**. Speak up as soon as you realise that your rights have been damaged. Look the person in the eye and keep your comments brief and to the point. *Example*: "It's about something that happened in the corridor today."

S stands for **Specific Behaviour**. What did the person do to damage your rights? Focus on the behaviour, not the person. Be as specific as you can. *Example*: "I didn't like it when you pushed me. I dropped my books, and you kicked them across the corridor."

E stands for **Effect on Me**. Share the feelings you experienced as a result of the person's behaviour. *Example*: "It was embarrassing, plus I was late for class. I had to wait for the corridor to clear before I could pick up my books."

R stands for **Response**. Wait for a response from the other person. He or she might try to brush you off with "What's the big deal?" or "Don't be a baby" or "Can't you take a joke?" or "So what?" Don't let it bother you. At least it's a response. On the other hand, the person might apologise.

T stands for **Terms**. Suggest a solution to the problem. *Example*: "I want you to stop bothering me in the corridor. If you don't, I'll report you to the teacher."

Tips: The ASSERT Formula may feel strange and awkward at first. It isn't foolproof, and it won't always work. In some situations – for example, bullying that involves physical violence – it might make things worse. And some bullies feed on getting *any* kind of response, even an assertive response. If your being assertive seems to anger or provoke the bully, walk away or run away.

WORK TOGETHER TO SOLVE A PROBLEM

When you and your pupils work together to solve a problem outside the classroom – when you face a common 'enemy' as a group – you naturally grow closer to each other in the process. This builds unity, acceptance and the satisfaction of joining forces for a good cause.

Ask your pupils to brainstorm specific problems they'd like to address. These might be problems in your school, your community or the world. (*Examples*: pollution, smoking, drugs, cruelty to animals, homelessness, hunger.) Write their ideas on the board. Afterwards, have pupils choose one to work on. You might ask for a show of hands or prepare secret ballots so pupils can vote for their top choices.

Once you've identified a problem, find ways for your pupils to take action and make a difference.

BUILD UNDERSTANDING

Why do bullies bully? Why do targets put up with it? There are no easy answers to these questions, but experts have identified reasons why some children become bullies and others become targets. Share this information with your pupils. It might help them understand why they and their classmates do some of the things they do, and it will also build empathy (see pages 50–51).

Some children bully . . .

. . . because they love having power. Most bullying is about having power over other people.

. . . because their parents/carers or other people bully them. They have learned by example that bullying is how bigger, stronger people relate to others and get their way.

. . . as a way to get attention.

. . . to make themselves look bigger or tougher than they really are – or they feel inside.

. . . because they are jealous of other people. They can't stand it when others are smarter, more popular or more successful than they are.

. . . to protect themselves from being picked on or criticised. They're afraid of being hurt, and they take out their fear on other people.

. . . because they enjoy hurting other people and making them feel afraid.

. . . because they don't know any better. They haven't learned how to make friends and get along with others.

. . . because they like to win, no matter what. They can't stand losing at anything.

. . . because they have their own problems and don't know how to cope. Maybe they're miserable at home. Maybe they know they don't fit in and other children don't like them. They take out their feelings on people who are weaker and unable to fight back.

Some children are targets . . .

. . . because they are 'different' in some way. They may be taller or shorter, heavier or thinner, wear braces, wear glasses, have a physical disability or a learning difference, 'talk funny', 'look funny', and on and on. Everyone is unique, so there are countless 'differences' bullies can identify and pick on.

. . . because they seem vulnerable – like 'easy targets'. Maybe they're passive, sensitive, quiet, shy, or stand out in some other way. For whatever reason, they look as if they can't or won't stick up for themselves.

. . . because they don't know how to make friends and get along with others. They're isolated, alone and lonely. They don't have people they can count on to come to their defence.

. . . because they're socially awkward. Maybe they say and do the 'wrong' things. Maybe they wear the 'wrong' clothes. For whatever reason, they don't fit in.

. . . as a way to get attention. They don't know how to seek positive attention, so they seek negative attention. They may act 'strange' or annoying.

. . . because they're bullies. How does this work? Imagine that a 10-year-old bullies children his (or her) age and younger. This person doesn't know how to make friends. He (or she) may be bossy, aggressive and rude. Now put that 10-year-old in a group of older children, and suddenly he (or she) isn't as big, strong or scary. Instead, he (or she) is a child who doesn't have friends, doesn't know how to act, and is suddenly very vulnerable.

Invite pupils to contribute their own reasons why some children are bullies and some are targets. Listen for any reasons that indicate acceptance of bullying behaviours or scorn for targets. If necessary, remind pupils that no one has the 'right' to be a bully or a 'good reason' to bully someone else. And no one 'deserves' to be a target.

SET AND REVIEW WEEKLY GOALS

Start each week with a brief discussion of how everyone can work together to create a positive classroom environment. Set specific goals everyone can agree on and work towards. For ideas, you might review your class rules (see 'Set Rules', pages' 33–34), acceptance statements (see 'Build Acceptance', pages 17–18), and/or pupils' ideas for making the classroom anti-bullying (see 'Designate Your Classroom Anti-Bullying', page 35). You might ask questions like these:

- What can we do this week so everyone feels safe, accepted and appreciated?

- What can we do to prevent bullying?

- How will we treat each other?

- How will we expect to be treated?

- What specific actions can help us all have a great week?

As pupils offer ideas, write them on the board. Try to summarise the ideas into a single, simple state-ment of goals. Leave it on the board for the entire week.

On Wednesday, review the goals statement with the pupils. Ask questions like:

- Are we meeting our goals as a class?

- Is there anything we need to work harder on?

On Friday, look back on the week. Ask questions like:

- Did we meet our goals this week?

- In general, how did people treat each other during the week?

- Did we all have a good week? Why or why not?

- What can we do next week to improve?

Invite pupils' ideas about ways to make your class-room even friendlier, more peaceful and more accepting. Use those ideas as starters for next week's goal-setting discussion.

Tip: For another approach, see 'Assess the Week' (page 76).

ASSIGN RELATED READING

Have pupils read and report on books about bully-ing, friendship, conflict and acceptance.* Discuss them as a class, or have pupils write original sto-ries featuring characters they encountered in the books. How would these characters handle a fight on the playground? A shoving match in the corri-dor? Teasing? Rejection? Hurt feelings? What else? Invite your pupils to come up with their own suggestions for situations they'd like to portray.

Reading and writing are reasonably non-threaten-ing ways to explore issues of friendship, rejection, prejudice, acceptance, conflict, bullying and other topics.

---

* See 'Books for Children' in 'Resources' (pages 145–151) for suggestions. You might also ask your school librarian or the children's librarian at your local public library to point you toward appropriate books.

TEACH CONFLICT RESOLUTION SKILLS

Conflict between people is normal and inevitable, and not all conflict is harmful or bad. *Destructive* conflict damages relationships, creates bad feelings and leads to future problems. But *constructive* conflict helps us learn, grow and change for the better. We see things from other perspectives. We become more open-minded, tolerant and accepting. We build stronger relationships with the people in our lives.

What makes the difference? How we choose to *manage* the conflicts we experience. It takes (at least) two people to start and sustain a conflict. If both agree to seek a positive resolution, half the battle is won.

Everyone benefits from learning and practising conflict resolution skills. Bullies discover the real power of solving problems without using force or intimidation. Targets are empowered to seek solutions instead of giving up and giving in. Your classroom becomes a place where people are willing to work together.

Conflict resolution isn't learned or taught in a day. There are many resources that look at conflict resolution in more detail than this book. The SEAL curriculum, for example, provides meaningful activities that aim to develop conflict resolution skills in children as just one part of a whole programme that develops emotional literacy, self-esteem, self-awareness, anger management...etc.

Note: Research shows that teaching conflict resolution *works*. Pupils who are not trained in conflict resolution are more likely to withdraw from conflicts or use force in conflict situations. Pupils who are trained in conflict resolution are more likely to face conflicts, use problem solving to negotiate solutions – and have a more positive attitude towards school in general.*

If you don't yet have access to any conflict resolution teaching materials, there's a basic approach you can teach your pupils right away. Distribute copies of the handout 'Eight Steps to Conflict Resolution' (page 65). Lead pupils through it step by step. Reinforce it with practice, role-plays, short plays or whatever you think will reach your pupils most effectively.

SET UP A PEACE PLACE

Set aside a corner of your classroom as the 'Peace Place'. Tell pupils they can go there when they need to resolve a conflict, talk to another pupil about a problem they're having, or just spend some quiet time when they're feeling upset, frustrated or overwhelmed.

Furnish your Peace Place with a small table or desk, two or three chairs (or cushions or bean-bags), peaceful posters (nature scenes, animals, people), a cassette player or two (with headphones) and cassettes of quiet music or nature sounds. Start and build a small library of appropriate books – on friendship, conflict resolution, peacefulness and related topics – and keep them in a bookcase in your Peace Place.

As a class, develop a set of short, simple rules for the Peace Place. Have pupils make and decorate a poster listing the rules. *Examples*:

1. **If you're having a problem with another pupil, ask him or her to go to the Peace Place with you and talk it over.**

2. **If another pupil asks you to go to the Peace Place, say yes.**

3. **When you're in the Peace Place, use gentle, respectful words.**

4. **Take turns talking and listening.**

5. **Use 'I messages' to communicate your wants, needs and feelings.***

6. **Be a good listener. Pay attention to what the other person says. Don't interrupt.**

7. **If you can't solve the problem on your own, ask the teacher for help.**

8. **The Peace Place is special. Keep it neat and clean.**

---

* SOURCE: *Review of Educational Research* 66:4 (1996), pp. 459–506.

* See 'Teach Students to Use "I Messages,"' page 55.

EIGHT STEPS TO CONFLICT RESOLUTION

1. **Cool down.** Don't try to resolve a conflict when you're angry (or the other person is angry). Take a time-out or agree to meet again in 24 hours.

2. **Describe the conflict.** Each person should tell about it in his or her own words. No put-downs allowed! *Important*: Although each person may have a different view of the conflict and use different words to describe it, neither account is 'right' or 'wrong'.

3. **Describe what caused the conflict.** What specific events led up to the conflict? What happened first? Next? Did the conflict start out as a minor disagreement or difference of opinion? What happened to turn it into a conflict? *Important*: Don't label the conflict either person's "fault."

4. **Describe the feelings raised by the conflict.** Again, each person should use his or her own words. Honesty is important. No blaming allowed!

5. **Listen carefully and respectfully while the other person is talking.** Try to understand his or her point of view. Don't interrupt. It might help to 'reflect' the other person's perceptions and feelings by repeating them back. *Examples*: "You didn't like it when I called you a name." "Your feelings are hurt." "You thought you should have first choice about what game to play at breaktime." "You're sad because you feel left out."

6. **Brainstorm solutions to the conflict.** Follow the three basic rules of brainstorming:

   - Everyone tries to come up with as many ideas as they can.

   - All ideas are okay.

   - Nobody makes fun of anyone else's ideas.

   Be creative. Affirm each other's ideas. Be open to new ideas. Make a list of brainstormed ideas so you're sure to remember them all. Then choose one solution to try. Be willing to negotiate and compromise.

7. **Try your solution.** See how it works. Give it your best efforts. Be patient.

8. **If one solution doesn't get results, try another.** Keep trying. Brainstorm more solutions if you need to.

If you can't resolve the conflict no matter how hard you try, agree to disagree. Sometimes that's the best you can do. Meanwhile, realise that the conflict doesn't have to end your relationship. People can get along even when they disagree.

EXPLORE THE LIVES OF FAMOUS PEACEMAKERS

Jane Addams. Amnesty International. Menachem Begin. His Holiness the Dalai Lama of Tibet. Mikhail Gorbachev. John Hume. The International Committee of the Red Cross. Martin Luther King Jr. Aung San Suu Kyi. Nelson Mandela. Mother Teresa. Linus Pauling. Yitzhak Rabin. Albert Schweitzer. David Trimble. Rigoberta Menchu Tum. Desmond Tutu. Lech Walesa. Betty Williams. Jody Williams. What do these people and organisations have in common? All are winners of the Nobel Peace Prize, perhaps the world's most revered and prestigious award.

Have pupils research a Nobel Peace Prize winner or another peacemaker they admire. To share what they learn, they might write brief biographies, present short plays, write songs, create collages or do another activity they choose.

Encourage them to look for answers to this question: "What did this person do that I can do, too?" Help students 'translate' their peacemakers' accomplishments into simple, inspiring statements. *Examples*:

- "1998 Nobel Peace Prize winners John Hume and David Trimble worked to find a peaceful solution to the conflict in Northern Ireland. I can be a peer mediator and help my classmates find solutions to their conflicts."

- "1992 Nobel Peace Prize winner Rigoberta Menchu Tum works for human rights. I can learn about the Universal Declaration of Human Rights and tell other people about it."

- "1984 Nobel Peace Prize winner Bishop Desmond Tutu worked against apartheid in South Africa. I can fight racism, bigotry and prejudice in my school and community."

TEACH PEER MEDIATION SKILLS

Your pupils can learn to help each other resolve conflicts through peer mediation. Mediators don't offer solutions. Instead, they ask open-ended questions, encourage discussion and guide people involved in a conflict to come up with and try their own solutions.

Identify pupils you believe would make good peer mediators. These will be pupils who can stay calm, listen carefully, remain objective, avoid taking sides and be patient, plus they should be genuinely interested in serving as peer mediators. Make it clear that this isn't a 'power position'. Explain that mediators are 'between' the people involved in a conflict, like the lines in the middle of a road. Their job is to help the two sides come together, not to impose solutions or take credit for solutions that work.

Peer mediators start by asking themselves seven important questions:*

- Am I the right person?

- Can I assist without taking sides?

- Will both parties let me assist?

- Is this the right time to intervene?

- Are the parties relatively calm?

- Do we have enough time?

- Is this the right place?

If pupils can answer yes to these questions, they're ready to try mediating the conflict. The 'Steps for Mediation' handout (page 67) can lead them through the process.

 Go further:
Some schools have developed peer mediation to deal with small problems that arise during break and lunch times. These schemes have evaluated well and have reduced the number of incidents that escalate to become serious. Check to see whether your local authority can provide support with setting up such a scheme.

I. INTRODUCTION

1. Introduce yourself as a mediator.
2. Ask those in the conflict if they would like your help in solving the problem.
3. Find a quiet area to hold the mediation.
4. Ask for agreement to the following:
   - try to solve the problem
   - no name-calling
   - let the other person finish talking
   - confidentiality.

II. LISTENING

5. Ask the first person "What happened?" Paraphrase.
6. Ask the first person how she or he feels. Reflect the feelings.
7. Ask the second person "What happened?" Paraphrase.
8. Ask the second person how he or she feels. Reflect the feelings.

III. LOOKING FOR SOLUTIONS

9. Ask the first person what she or he could have done differently. Paraphrase.
10. Ask the second person what she or he could have done differently. Paraphrase.
11. Ask the first person what she or he can do here and now to help solve the problem. Paraphrase.
12. Ask the second person what she or he can do here and now to help solve the problem. Paraphrase.
13. Use creative questioning to bring both sides closer to a solution.

IV. FINDING SOLUTIONS

14. Help both sides find a solution they feel good about.
15. Repeat the solution and all of its parts to both sides and ask whether each agrees.
16. Congratulate both people on a successful mediation.

Caution: Peer mediation will not be suitable for dealing with all situations or with all pupils. Bullies have (and want) power over their targets. Targets may have low (or no) communication or assertiveness skills, especially in the bullies' presence. Targets might be intimidated and afraid because of past bullying incidents and worried about future retaliation, both of which can stand in the way of talking honestly, listening openly and feeling free to suggest possible solutions. You may want to reserve peer mediation for minor fall-outs or other types of conflict.

CHANGE SEATING ARRANGEMENTS

If you let pupils sit wherever they like, it may happen that the shy and lonely children, bullying targets or potential targets gravitate towards the outer edges of the class. It may also happen that the aggressive children, bullies or potential bullies sit towards the back, where their behaviour is less likely to be noticed by you.

Take a look at where pupils are sitting. What do you see? Bring the shy and lonely 'outsiders' into the centre of the class, where they will have more opportunities to interact with other pupils. (Don't put them next to each other, or they'll mostly interact with each other.) Bring the aggressive children up front, where you can keep a closer eye on them.

Change the seating arrangements in your classroom periodically so pupils can get to know a variety of people.

SAY CHEESE!

Keep a camera close at hand. Routinely take pictures of your pupils working together, playing together and interacting with each other in positive ways. Then:

- Post the pictures on your classroom bulletin board. Go ahead and fill it up with lots of pictures over the next several months; don't worry about overcrowding.

Or . . .

- Display the pictures in an oversized class photo album. Leave it out on a shelf or a corner of your desk so pupils can look through it often.

When pupils see themselves in pictures with each other, this gives them a sense of belonging to the group. (This is one reason why sports coaches take team pictures.) When you keep the pictures together in one place, this sends a message of unity and acceptance.

You'll probably notice that your pupils love looking at the pictures and discussing them with visitors. Don't be surprised if they're a special attraction on Parents' Evening and at open houses.

 Go further:
Take the camera with you on school trips and to school events. Capture some action shots of pupils involved in projects, presentations and sporting events. Schedule a 'photo shoot' and encourage pupils to create their own scenes of classroom harmony and cooperation.

Note: With this suggestion you will, of course, need to be mindful of any parents/carers who have expressed a wish for their child not to be filmed or photographed.

TEACH PUPILS ABOUT PEER PRESSURE AND INFLUENCE

Children and young people are undoubtedly influenced by their peers. This is never more true than when they reach upper primary and lower secondary school. Peer influence can be positive (e.g. encouraging someone to take part in a sports event) but it can also make children and young people do things they don't really want to do because they are scared to be perceived as different or of 'not fitting in'.

Discuss the following questions with your class to explore the idea of peer influence:

- If everyone in your class except you turned up one day wearing bright yellow socks, how would you feel? What makes you feel like this?

- Have you ever done anything just because everyone else was doing it – even if you didn't really want to?

- Why are people sometimes scared to be different?

- What do people really think about a person who sticks up for themselves and only does things that they really want to do?

Direct, negative peer pressure is not actually that common. The stereotype of a young person trying to pressurise another into doing something harmful or dangerous (e.g. smoke) that is often used in resources can exaggerate the likelihood of this situation actually happening. Make pupils aware that the best response to being pressurised into doing something your gut reaction is telling you not to do is to be assertive. For example:

- Stay calm and cool

- Be confident (stand tall with head up and shoulders straight) and try not to look scared

- Avoid arguing

- Politely say "no thanks" to any offers (don't believe you'll be more popular or tougher if you say "yes").

 Go further:
Ask pupils what they think they would do if they saw a friend picking on someone else. Peer influence might encourage them to join in. Ask pupils to consider the choices they have in this situation.

TRACK BULLYING ON TV

We already know that pupils are exposed to a great deal of violence on television. According to the American Psychological Association, research has shown that TV violence affects children negatively in three major ways:

- Children may become less sensitive to the pain and suffering of others.

- They may become more fearful of the world around them and perceive it as a mean and dangerous place.

- They may become more likely to behave aggressively towards others.

Studies have shown that children's television shows contain about 20 violent acts each hour. It's likely that many of your pupils also watch programmes aimed at adult audiences, where the violent content can be frequent, graphic and realistic.

Bullying is a form of violence against others. Whether physical (hitting, kicking, pushing) or emotional (rejection, put-downs, threats), it can leave targets feeling powerless and abused.

Tell your pupils that you want them to track bullying on TV for one week. As they watch their regular programmes, they should pay special attention to bullying behaviours. Give each pupil several copies of the handout 'Bullying on TV' (page 70); have more copies available as needed throughout the week. Explain that pupils should use one handout per programme to report on the bullying they see. They should bring each night's handouts to school the next day and give them to you. Review them as they come in to get an overall sense of your pupils' TV viewing habits and how much bullying they notice.

If you and your pupils did the 'Define Bullying' activity (page 17) and the 'Name Bullying Behaviours' activity (pages 21 and 23), everyone should have a general idea of what these behaviours include. If you didn't do these activities, take a few moments to introduce the main ideas. Make sure everyone understands that bullying encompasses a broad spectrum of behaviours.

At the end of the week, return each pupil's handouts and have a class discussion about bullying on TV. You might ask questions like these:

- How much bullying did you see on TV? None? A little? A lot?

Over to you

BULLYING ON TV

Today's date: _____

Your name: _____

Name of the TV programme you watched: _____

What channel was it on? _____

Did you notice any bullying?   yes ☐   no ☐

If *yes*, describe what happened: _____

_____

_____

How did the bullying affect the target? _____

_____

_____

What did the target do about the bullying? _____

_____

_____

What, if anything, happened to the bully? _____

_____

_____

Did it seem that:

    the target deserved to be bullied?   yes ☐   no ☐

    the bullying was the target's fault?   yes ☐   no ☐

- What kinds of bullying did you see?

- Which kinds seemed to be most common?

- Experts believe that watching violence on TV is bad for children. Do you think that watching bullying on TV might be bad for children, too? Why or why not?

- In general, when bullying happens on TV, do the bullies get away with it? Do the targets get hurt? Does it seem as if the bullying is the targets' fault?

- Now that you've watched for bullying on TV, how do you feel about it? What's your opinion?

Go further:
If pupils are concerned about the amount of bullying they see on TV, have them write letters to the channel or programme expressing their opinions about specific programmes. Addresses and contact details can usually be found on the Internet.

AFFIRM YOUR PUPILS

Everyone appreciates a compliment. Pupils especially enjoy knowing that their teacher thinks well of them. Take every opportunity to say something positive to each of your pupils throughout the day. Your comments should be brief, honest, sincere, simple and *specific*. *Examples*: "Christopher, I liked the way you helped Maria find her pencil." "Abby, I really appreciate your positive attitude today." "Kai, you did a great job on the reading assignment."

POSITIVE POSTERS
Provide each pupil with a sheet of A4 plain paper and ask them to write and decorate their name in the middle of it. Ask pupils to add more personal details to their sheet such as a cartoon picture of themselves, a list of their favourite things, a picture of their house etc. but explain that they do need to leave plenty of space on the page for someone to write. Take the sheets in. Over the next week or so, write personalised compliments

on each pupil's sheet. You could write about anything in particular you noticed a pupil do well in addition to compliments about their personality – which could include some of the qualities from the following list.

Go further:
Ask pupils to brainstorm compliments that could be given to other people (e.g. "I like spending time with you", "You are fun"... etc.) and display them in the classroom to encourage their use.

- able to resolve conflicts
- alert
- ambitious
- analytical
- appreciative
- articulate
- assertive
- attentive
- aware
- calm
- careful
- caring
- cautious
- cheerful
- confident
- conscientious
- consistent
- cooperative
- courageous
- courteous
- creative
- dedicated
- dependable
- determined
- dynamic
- eager
- efficient
- empathetic
- energetic
- enthusiastic
- ethical
- fair
- faithful
- focused
- friendly
- fun
- generous
- gentle
- genuine
- giving
- goal setter
- good example
- good follower
- good listener
- good sport
- hard-working
- health-conscious
- healthy
- helpful
- honest
- honourable
- hopeful
- humble
- humorous
- imaginative
- independent
- industrious
- ingenious
- innovative
- inspiring
- intelligent
- interesting
- intuitive
- inventive
- kind

- knowledgeable
- leader
- likable
- likes people
- lively
- logical
- loving
- loyal
- mature
- mediator
- merry
- motivated
- neat
- nice
- obedient
- open-minded
- optimistic
- organised
- patient
- peaceful
- people-oriented
- perceptive
- persevering
- planner
- pleasant
- polite
- positive
- precise
- problem solver
- punctual
- quick
- reasonable
- relaxed
- reliable
- reputable
- resilient
- resourceful
- responsible
- safety-conscious
- self-assured
- self-disciplined
- sensible
- sensitive
- sharing
- sincere
- spirited
- stable
- strong
- successful
- tactful
- tender-hearted
- thoughtful
- tolerant
- trusting
- trustworthy
- understanding
- unselfish
- upbeat
- versatile
- willing to compromise
- wise
- witty

TEACH PUPILS TO AFFIRM THEMSELVES

Provide pupils with small blank books or notebooks (or put these on your list of school supplies to send home to parents at the start of the school year). Have them label their books "What's Good About Me" and use them to list and describe their positive characteristics. Get them started by asking questions like these:

- What do you like about yourself?

- What are you good at? Best at?

- What are your positive characteristics?

- What good things would you like other people to know about you?

- What makes you proud of yourself?

You might also refer to the list of starter words in 'Affirm Your Pupils' (page 71 and above).

 Go further:
Allow other people (pupils, teachers, visiting parents, teaching assistants etc.) to add their own comments to pupils' books. To ensure that comments are positive, set two rules: 1) Everyone must sign his or her comment(s). 2) No one may write in another person's book without his or her permission.

Every so often, you might ask a pupil if it's okay to read aloud from his or her book. If it is, choose a few comments to share with the class. This encourages pupils to recognise and acknowledge each other's positive characteristics and notice similarities.

It's likely that these books will become cherished possessions – something your pupils will treasure for many years.

For more ways to help children learn to affirm themselves, see 'Teach Positive Self-Talk' (pages 76 and 77).

TEACH PUPILS TO AFFIRM EACH OTHER

When pupils affirm each other, everyone feels accepted, appreciated and valued. Here are six approaches you can try with your pupils.

AFFIRMATIONS BOX
Take a box with a lid (a large shoebox works well) and cut a slit in the top. Decorate it (or have pupils decorate it). Label it the 'Affirmations Box' and put it on a shelf or a corner of your desk.

Invite pupils to write positive statements about each other whenever they like and drop them in the box. Once a week, once a day or whenever you choose, dip into the box, pull out a statement or two and read it aloud to the class.

This is a powerful way to encourage pupils to notice and appreciate each other's positive qualities. It helps them to see qualities they might have overlooked and discover similarities.

AFFIRMATIONS CARDS

Write each pupil's name on an index card. Hand out the cards randomly (just make sure that no one gets his or her own name). Then have each pupil write something positive about the pupil named on the card. *Examples*: "Sara is a terrific soccer player." "Ren is always willing to help." "Zach tells the best jokes." "Ashley has a great smile." Explain that you need them to take this seriously, because you (or they) will be reading their statements aloud. Ask pupils to sign their statements. (Anyone who's tempted to write something negative will think twice if his or her signature is on the card.)

Give the class a few minutes to write their statements. Collect them and review them quickly to make absolutely sure that all statements are positive. Then hand them back to the pupils and invite volunteers to read their statements aloud. If a pupil isn't comfortable doing this in front of the class, you can offer to read his or her statement. Either way, everyone should enjoy the experience.

Do this several times during the school year – once a week or once a month.

 Go further:
Take individual photos of your pupils and display them on a bulletin board along with their positive statements. Teachers who have done this report that pupils visit the bulletin board often, reading the statements and pointing out similar positive comments.

Note: With this suggestion you will, of course, need to be mindful of any parents/carers who have expressed a wish for their child not to be filmed or photographed.

AFFIRMATIONS CIRCLES

Divide the class into two groups. (If you have an uneven number of pupils, join this activity yourself.) Have one group form a circle facing inwards. Have the other group form a circle around the first group. Each pupil in the outer circle should stand directly behind a pupil in the inner circle.

On your cue, each pupil in the outer circle whispers a positive, encouraging statement in that pupil's ear. The statement should be brief, honest, sincere and simple. *Examples*: "I like the way you draw." "Thanks for helping me study for the maths test." "I see you got your hair cut. It looks great." "I think you're the friendliest person in the class." "I'm glad you're my friend."

Next, have the pupils in the outer circle move one person to the left (or the right) and do it again (give a positive statement). Keep going until the outer circle has moved all the way around the inner circle. Then have the circles switch places – the outer circle becomes the inner circle, and pupils who have been giving positive statements now have the chance to receive them.

Afterwards, talk about the activity. Ask: "How did it feel to *say* something positive to another person?" "How did it feel to *hear* someone make a positive, encouraging statement about you?"

THUMBS UP

When one pupil makes a negative 'thumbs down' comment about another, immediately ask him or her to make two positive 'thumbs up' comments about that person. If the pupil has difficulty doing this (or won't do it), ask the class to make the positive comments. *Tip*: If you did the 'Positive Poster' activity (pages 71–72), you can have one pupil read what you wrote about the pupil who was the target of the 'thumbs down'.

Encourage your pupils to use a 'thumbs up' sign in class, in the playground, in the dining hall, in the corridors and elsewhere to show their approval and support for each other.

Good for You!

_____ **did something special.**
(Student's name)

Here's what _____ **did:**
(name)

Today's date: _____

Your name: _____

MY WEEK AT SCHOOL

Today's date: _____

Your name (if you want to give it): _____

Think back on the past week in this classroom. Read each statement, then tick the column that best describes how you feel about your week.

This week in school:	All of the time	Most of the time	Some of the time	Never
1. I was respected as a person.				
2. I treated others with respect.				
3. I was treated fairly.				
4. I treated others fairly.				
5. People helped me when I needed help.				
6. I helped others.				
7. We cared for each other.				
8. We worked hard to make our classroom a positive place to be.				
9. I felt like I belonged.				
10. I helped others feel like they belonged.				
11. I was encouraged to do my best.				
12. I encouraged others to do their best.				
13. We worked together to solve problems.				
14. We cooperated with each other.				
15. I felt accepted.				
16. I helped others feel accepted.				

APPLAUSE, APPLAUSE!

Invite your pupils to show their approval of a class-mate's performance, good deed or other positive action in a time-honoured way: with applause. Encourage them to applaud vigorously and often.

You might say, "We applaud – or clap – people to let them know we like something they're doing or something they've done. We enjoy it when people clap us, and they enjoy it when we clap them." Ask pupils to suggest times when they might applaud each other.

Have a brief practice session and set some ground rules so pupils don't get carried away with this. For example, they should stop clapping on a signal from you – perhaps when you raise your hand. You might create an "APPLAUSE!" sign or banner for your classroom. Point to the sign or banner to remind pupils to applaud when it's appropriate.

GOOD FOR YOU! CERTIFICATES

Once a week or twice a month, ask pupils to cele-brate each other's achievements and accomplish-ments by completing 'Good for You!' certificates (page 74). Explain that the achievements and accomplishments can be large or small, and they don't necessarily have to happen in the classroom or even be school-related.

Keep several copies of the certificate on hand. Post completed certificates around the classroom for a few days, then allow the honoured pupils to take them down and take them home to share with their families. *Tip*: Make sure that *all* pupils are recognised often, not just the same few pupils. Fill out certificates yourself for pupils whose achieve-ments and accomplishments might otherwise go unnoticed.

ASSESS THE WEEK

According to an old saying, "Before we can decide where we're going, we have to know where we've been." End each week by inviting your pupils to reflect on the events of that week. Distribute copies of the handout 'My Week at School' (page 75). Tally the results (or ask a volunteer to do this) and report them on Monday morning. Use the results to set goals or objectives for the coming week.

Tip: For another approach, see 'Set and Review Weekly Goals' (page 63).

WEAR ANTI-BULLYING BADGES

Have pupils design and make buttons or badges with a "No Bullying!" message. They might say "No Bullying!" or "No Bullying Allowed!" or "Anti-Bullying Action!" or whatever pupils prefer. You could laminate the badges and stick safety pins on the backs, use a badge making machine or pay to have the badges made up properly.

TEACH POSITIVE SELF-TALK

It's no secret that positive thinking can be power-ful – especially positive thinking about ourselves and our abilities to solve problems, reach goals, cope with hard times and accomplish what we set out to do. Positive self-talk creates positive beliefs. Positive beliefs lead to positive attitudes and feelings about oneself and others. Positive attitudes and feelings promote positive behav-iours.

Successful, capable, competent people tend to be self-affirmers. They don't get carried away ("I'm the greatest!"), but they do give themselves fre-quent pep talks ("I can do it!").

Many pupils who are bullied – and even those who aren't – have difficulty with this. It's easy for them to lapse into negative self-talk ("I can't do it," "Why even try?"), which can set the stage for neg-ative beliefs, attitudes, feelings and behaviours – and also for failure, which 'proves' that their neg-ative self-talk was right.

There are many ways to teach positive self-talk. Here are six you can explore with your pupils:

1. Have a class discussion about self-talk, both positive and negative. Make sure pupils know

the difference. Give examples or ask them for examples. Explain that positive self-talk *really works*.

2. Hand out copies of 'Messages from Me to Me' (page 78), which lists several brief statements pupils can use in their positive self-talk. Read it aloud or invite pupils to read individual statements. Suggest that pupils keep the list and refer to it often.

Go further:

Have pupils pick two or three statements from the list, write them on an index card, and carry the card with them in their pocket or backpack. Or they can write their own statements.

3. Have pupils write brief positive self-talk scripts to keep in their notebooks or at their desks. (*Example*: "I know I can do this. I have the ability. If I get stuck, I can ask for help. I can succeed.") When pupils catch themselves using negative self-talk (or when anyone else catches them), they can read their scripts. The briefer the better; after a few readings, many pupils will have their scripts memorised. Suggest that they close their eyes and take a few deep breaths before repeating their scripts to themselves.

4. Before starting a new class activity, ask pupils to close their eyes and silently say one or two positive statements to themselves. Or you might write statements on the board and say them aloud as a class.

5. Divide the class into small groups. Have each group come up with a list of negative self-talk statements, then brainstorm positive self-talk responses. Afterwards, the groups can share their lists with the class.

6. Have pupils complete 'Good for You!' certificates for themselves, describing their own achievements and accomplishments. See 'Teach Pupils to Affirm Each Other', pages 72–73 and 76.

USE HUMOUR

Humour is a terrific tool for making everyone feel welcome, accepted and appreciated. Laughter is good for us *physically* (increasing respiratory activity, oxygen exchange, muscular activity and heart rate; stimulating the cardiovascular system and sympathetic nervous system; leading to an overall positive biochemical state) and *mentally* (decreasing stress, lifting spirits, improving moods). Here are six ways to bring humour and laughter into your classroom:

1. Start each day with a joke or two. You might have pupils bring in their favourite jokes to share.

2. For a special treat now and then, show a funny film.

3. Start a class collection of joke books and cartoon books.

4. Have a 'Humour Corner' in your classroom. Stock it with funny books, posters, audiotapes and other resources.

5. Keep a 'Joke Jar' in your classroom. Fill it with brief jokes written on small pieces of paper. Encourage pupils to contribute their own jokes. (Set a few ground rules first: No hurtful jokes. No biased jokes. No crude or tasteless jokes.) Once a day, you (or a pupil) can reach into the jar, pull out a joke, and share it with the class.

6. Read humorous stories aloud or give them as reading assignments.

Talk with your class about the difference between laughing *at* someone and laughing *with* someone. Ask questions like these:

- When is it okay to laugh?

- When is it not okay to laugh?

- Are there times when laughter can hurt? How can it hurt?

- Are there times when laughter can help? How can it help?

"I'm a good person."

"I deserve to be treated with kindness and respect."

"I'm special and unique."

"I'm creative and talented."

"I can set goals and reach them."

"I can solve problems."

"I can ask other people for help."

"I have a right to be imperfect."

"I have a right to make mistakes."

"Everyone makes mistakes."

"I can learn from my mistakes."

"I'm valuable and worthwhile . . . just the way I am."

"I can get through this."

"I'm learning and growing."

"I'm not alone."

"I'm okay."

"I'm strong and capable."

"Even if I don't feel so great right now, I'll feel better soon."

"I can be patient with myself."

"I can manage."

"I can cope."

"I can do this."

"I can succeed."

"I can try again."

"I can expect the best of myself."

"I'm brave and courageous."

"I believe in myself."

"I'm not afraid."

MONITOR THE MESSAGES YOU SEND

Children – even very young children – are amazingly perceptive. They know when a pupil is the 'teacher's pet'. They can tell when a teacher dislikes a pupil or doubts the pupil's abilities to learn and get along with others.

How can you make sure you're sending the right 'messages' to your pupils? Consider the following suggestions. Ask other teachers about what has and hasn't worked for them. When you share strategies, experiences and insights, everyone benefits – you, your colleagues and pupils in your school.

1. Greet each pupil by name as he or she enters your classroom.

2. Each day, let every pupil know you care about him or her – in your words, body language and actions.

3. Make frequent eye contact with every pupil. Studies have shown that some teachers favour children they perceive as attractive. They make eye contact more often with those pupils, and they give them more positive attention, reinforcement, affirmations and feedback. They may call on those pupils more frequently.

4. Children have a strong need to appear successful in front of their peers and a deep fear of looking foolish or being laughed at. Plan and arrange classroom activities so all of your pupils can show their strengths, not their weaknesses. *Examples*: Avoid asking poor readers to read aloud to the class. If you know that a particular pupil has weak maths skills, don't insist that he or she work on problems on the board.

5. Show interest in every pupil. This is a powerful motivator and helps all pupils feel welcome, appreciated and accepted.

6. Be a good listener. Try to find time each day to really *listen* to each pupil. Lean forward, paraphrase their comments and communicate your understanding of what they're saying and feeling.

7. As much as possible, individualise your teaching strategies and assignments. Research indicates that individualised instruction decreases antisocial behaviours in the classroom. It also increases the chances that your pupils will succeed.

8. Write personal, positive notes and letters to your pupils throughout the year. Pupils love getting letters from their teachers. Before the start of the school year, consider sending letters to each of your future pupils, welcoming them to your class and hinting at some of what you'll be learning throughout the year. This can also help decrease some of their anxiety about the coming year.

9. Even though some pupils will be smarter, friendlier, better behaved and more likable than others, make sure they don't become 'teacher's pets'. Children are sensitive to favouritism and may be jealous of 'pets'. Jealousy can lead to bullying.

10. Do your best to treat all of your pupils equally. Avoid giving special privileges to some pupils and not others. This can create envy and hostility, which in turn can lead to bullying. If a pupil requires special treatment (for example because of a medical condition), make sure the rest of the class understands why. (Get the permission of the pupil and his or her parents first to avoid embarrassment and potential problems.)

11. Remind your pupils that 'equal' doesn't mean 'the same'. Explain that you'll do your very best to give everyone equal opportunities to learn and grow, but they will learn and grow in different ways.

12. When pupils see you put your trust in someone, they tend to have more respect for that person – especially if they respect you. Is there someone who seems to be having a hard time in school? Someone who's being picked on, excluded, teased or bullied? Plan an activity (in class or on a field trip) where you can demonstrate complete trust in that

pupil. When other pupils see this, they may view the pupil in a more positive light.

13. It's a real challenge to like every pupil all the time. Do your best to be accepting, sensitive and understanding even in difficult situations. Don't hide your feelings, but express them in positive, helpful ways. Give pupils a chance to respond. *Example*: "I'm disappointed that you didn't finish your maths homework. What can we do to keep this from happening again?"

14. We all have biases and prejudices. Some are based on cultural or ethnic background, others on gender, religion, intelligence or ability level. Examine your own prejudices. How did you come to learn or believe these things? Are they part of your daily life? Are they affecting your teaching? Are they having a negative effect on your pupils? Be honest with yourself. Make a conscious, deliberate, focused effort to check your prejudices, unlearn them and get beyond them.

15. Smile, smile, smile. Show your pupils that you're glad to be their teacher. This may be the most obvious positive message you can send.

16. Think positive thoughts about all of your pupils. Wish them the best in everything they do and have high hopes for them.

Helping targets

If you were bullied as a child, you can probably remember how you felt. You may recall the specifics of each incident – the people, places, words, insults, frustration, pain, anger and powerlessness.

The good news is: your pupils don't have to endure the bullying you put up with when you were their age. We know more about bullying now than we did ten or even five years ago, and we know more about how to prevent it and stop it. We know more about how to help the targets of bullying – and why we should and must.

The 'Creating a Positive Classroom' section of this book includes many tips and strategies that can benefit targets and potential targets. *Examples:*

- 'Teach Anger Management Skills' (page 35)

- 'Teach Friendship Skills' (pages 36, 39 and 41)

- 'Explore Ways to Deal with Bullies' (page 45)

- 'Use a Notes-to-the-Teacher Box' (pages 45–46)

- 'Teach Pupils to Use "I Messages"' (page 55)

- 'Teach Assertiveness Skills' (pages 57 and 60)

- 'Teach Conflict Resolution Skills' (page 64)

- 'Teach Pupils to Affirm Themselves' (page 72)

- 'Teach Positive Self-Talk' (pages 76–77)

Similarly, 'Helping Targets' features suggestions that you can use with all of your pupils. But most focus on pupils who desperately need adults to notice them, see what they're going through and do something about it.

As you try these ideas with your class, individual pupils and small groups, and as you share them with other teachers and staff, here are some good things you can expect to happen:

Your pupils will learn how to:

- stick up for themselves and each other
- developing a culture of telling and report bullying incidents
- differentiate between reporting and telling on someone
- feel stronger, more confident and better about themselves
- strengthen their bully resistance skills
- build their social skills
- plan ahead to avoid potential problems
- use humour and other 'power skills' to disarm bullies.

You'll discover how to:

- identify targets or potential targets
- encourage pupils to report bullying
- act quickly and effectively when you learn of a bullying incident
- communicate with parents and get them involved in making your classroom antibullying
- mobilise the masses – witnesses and bystanders – to become bully busters
- help pupils accept their differences
- equalise the power between targets and bullies
- protect yourself.

BE ALERT

Most bullying takes place where you (and other adults) can't see it or hear it. Bullies need an audience of their peers to establish their power over the target, but the last thing they want is an audience of adults who have power over *them* and can make them stop.

Pay attention to interactions between your pupils. Are there some who seem fearful, withdrawn, lonely and shy? Are there others who seem especially aggressive, need to 'win' all the time, seek excessive attention and are always pushing the boundaries of school or class rules? How do they get along with each other? What happens when they're seated beside each other, or are assigned to the same groups and expected to work together? Be watchful and alert.

Talk with your Midday Supervisory Assistant, monitors, playground supervisors, gym teachers and other adults who spend time with your pupils. Ask for their insights and input into relationships between your pupils. What have they seen? What have they heard? Learn as much as you can. It may be that bullying has gone on behind your back (even under your nose) and you simply haven't noticed it. If so, you're not alone.

IDENTIFY TARGETS OR POTENTIAL TARGETS

You may know that some pupils in your classroom are targets of bullying – because you've witnessed bullying events personally, or other students have reported them to you, or the targets themselves have come forward.

But most bullying goes unnoticed and unreported. How can you identify targets or potential targets? You can watch for specific behaviours – and you can seek input from pupils' parents.

 Important:
Experts have determined that there are two types of target:

- *passive targets* – anxious, sensitive loners who give off 'target' signals, lack self-defence skills, don't think quickly on their feet and have few friends to support them

- *provocative targets* – easily aroused, impulsive, annoying children who tease or taunt bullies, egg them on and make themselves targets but can't defend themselves.

LOOK FOR WARNING SIGNS
For any pupil you suspect might be a target or potential target, complete the 'Warning Signs' checklist (pages 83–84).

WARNING SIGNS

The following behaviours may indicate that a pupil is being bullied or is at risk of being bullied. For any pupil you're concerned about, tick all that apply.

When any of these behaviours are evident and persistent over time, you should definitely investigate. There's no magic number of warning signs that indicate a pupil is definitely being victimised – but it's better to be wrong than to allow a pupil to suffer.

Some of these characteristics are obviously more serious than others. A child who talks about suicide or carries a weapon to school, for example, needs *immediate* help. Don't wait for the child to come to you (this may never happen). Following the guidelines established by your school or local authority, contact a professional who is specially trained in dealing with high-risk behaviours.

Today's date: _____

Student's name: _____

SCHOOL AND SCHOOL WORK

_____	**1.**	Sudden change in school attendance/academic performance
_____	**2.**	Erratic attendance
_____	**3.**	Loss of interest in school work/academic performance/homework
_____	**4.**	Decline in quality of school work/academic performance*
_____	**5.**	Academic success; appears to be the teacher's pet*
_____	**6.**	Difficulty concentrating in class, easily distracted
_____	**7.**	Goes to break late and comes back early
_____	**8.**	Has a learning disability or difference
_____	**9.**	Lack of interest in school activities/events
_____	**10.**	Drops out of school activities he or she enjoys

SOCIAL

_____	**1.**	Lonely, withdrawn, isolated
_____	**2.**	Poor or no social/interpersonal skills
_____	**3.**	No friends or fewer friends than other pupils, unpopular, often/always picked last or groups or teams
_____	**4.**	Lacks a sense of humour, uses inappropriate humour
_____	**5.**	Often made fun of, laughed at, picked on, teased, put down and/or called names by other pupils, doesn't stand up for himself or herself
_____	**6.**	Often pushed around, kicked and/or hit by other pupils, doesn't defend himself or herself
_____	**7.**	Uses 'victim' body language – hunches shoulders, hangs head, won't look people in the eye, backs off from others

* True, numbers 4 and 5 are opposite. They are also extremes. Watch for any extremes or sudden changes; these can be signs that something stressful is happening in a pupil's life.

→ CONTINUED

_____ **8.** Has a noticeable difference that sets him or her apart from peers

_____ **9.** Comes from a racial, cultural, ethnic and/or religious background that puts him or her in the minority

_____ **10.** Prefers the company of adults during lunch and other free times

_____ **11.** Teases, pesters and irritates others, eggs them on, doesn't know when to stop

_____ **12.** Suddenly starts bullying other pupils

PHYSICAL

_____ **1.** Frequent illness*

_____ **2.** Frequent complaints of headache, stomachache, pains etc.*

_____ **3.** Scratches, bruises, damage to clothes or belongings etc. that don't have obvious explanations

_____ **4.** Sudden stammer or stutter

_____ **5.** Has a physical disability

_____ **6.** Has a physical difference that sets him/her apart from peers, e.g. wears glasses, is overweight/underweight, taller/shorter than peers, talks in an unusual way etc.

_____ **7.** Change in eating patterns, sudden loss of appetite

_____ **8.** Clumsy, uncoordinated, poor at sports

_____ **9.** Smaller than peers

_____ **10.** Physically weaker than peers

EMOTIONAL/BEHAVIOURAL

_____ **1.** Sudden change in mood or behaviour

_____ **2.** Passive, timid, quiet, shy, sullen, withdrawn

_____ **3.** Low or no self-confidence/self-esteem

_____ **4.** Low or no assertiveness skills

_____ **5.** Overly sensitive, cautious, clingy

_____ **6.** Nervous, anxious, worried, fearful, insecure

_____ **7.** Cries easily and/or often, becomes emotionally distraught, has extreme mood swings

_____ **8.** Irritable, disruptive, aggressive, quick-tempered, fights back (but always loses)

_____ **9.** Blames himself or herself for problems/difficulties

_____ **10.** Overly concerned about personal safety; spends a lot of time and effort thinking/worrying about getting safely to and from lunch, the toilets, lockers, through breaktime etc.; avoids certain places at school

_____ **11.** Talks about running away

_____ **12.** Talks about suicide

* A school nurse can determine whether these physical symptoms might have other causes. A nurse can also gently question a child to learn whether he/she is being bullied.

GET PARENTS' AND CARERS' INPUT

If a pupil shows some or many of the warning signs, it might be appropriate to contact the parents and arrange a face-to-face meeting at school.

No parent wants to hear that his or her child might be a target or potential target of bullying, so you'll need to offer a lot of reassurance along the way. You might start by emphasising your commitment to making your classroom anti-bullying. Share information about schoolwide efforts to reduce and eliminate bullying. Then tell the parents that you've noticed some behaviours at school which may indicate their child is being bullied or is a potential target of bullying. Give examples. Explain that there are other behaviours that don't show up at school, and you need their help identifying those behaviours.

Ask whether they have noticed any of the following in their child:

- Frequent illness*

- Frequent complaints of headache, stomachache, pains etc.*

- Sudden changes in behaviour (bed-wetting, nail-biting, tics, problems sleeping, loss of appetite, depression, crying, nightmares, stammering, stuttering etc.)*

- Seems anxious, fearful, moody, sad; refuses to say what's wrong

- Doesn't want to go to school, refuses to go to school, starts skipping school

- Changes walking route to school, wants to change buses, begs to be driven to school (refuses to walk or ride bus)

- Comes home from school with scratches, bruises, damage to clothes or belongings etc. that don't have obvious explanations; makes improbable excuses

- Comes home from school hungry (lunch money was "lost" or stolen)

- Possessions (books, money, clothing etc.) are often 'lost', damaged or destroyed

- Frequently asks for extra money (for lunch, school supplies etc.)

- Carries or wants to carry 'protection' (guns, knives, forks, sticks etc.) to school

- Sudden loss of interest in homework, school work, academic performance

- Has few or no friends; is rarely invited to parties or other social events

- Seems happy/normal on weekends but not during the week; seems preoccupied/tense on Sundays before school

- Obsesses about his or her height, weight, appearance, clothes etc.

- Has started bullying other children/siblings; is aggressive, rebellious, unreasonable

- Talks about running away or attempts to run away from home

- Talks about or attempts suicide.*

Keep a written record of your meeting and any relevant information the parents share with you. Thank the parents for coming in and talking to you. Tell them that you'll communicate with them often about their child's behaviour and progress, and about your efforts to make sure the bullying stops (or never starts). Then be sure to follow through.

TALK TO OTHER TEACHERS AND STAFF

If you think that a pupil is being bullied or might be at risk, share your concerns with other teachers or staff members.

If the pupil spends part of the day in another classroom, talk to that teacher. How is the pupil

---

* Ask the parents whether their child has been seen by a doctor recently; if not, suggest that they make an appointment. A doctor can determine whether these symptoms and behaviours might have other causes. A doctor can also gently question a child to learn whether he or she is being bullied.

---

* If parents report this behaviour, urge them to seek professional help *immediately*. Follow the guidelines established by your school or local authority.

treated by other children in the class? Has the teacher noticed any sudden changes in the pupil's behaviour? (See 'Identify Targets or Potential Targets', pages 82 and 85.) Has the pupil said anything about feeling worried, anxious or afraid to be in school?

Talk to a playground supervisor to find out how the pupil is treated at breaktime. If the pupil takes the bus to and from school, talk to the bus driver.

Other adults may be aware of events in the pupil's life that could indicate a bullying situation. You might also discover that problems you've noticed are not isolated incidents. If so, find out more and follow through.

EXAMINE YOUR OWN BELIEFS

To help targets gain the strength and skills to stop being targets, to help bullies change their behaviour, and to reduce or reduce the chances of bullying in your classroom, you need to believe that bullying is a problem that can be identified, addressed and resolved.

Since you're reading this book, chances are you're already convinced. But many adults (including teachers) have lingering misconceptions about bullying. It's worth taking the time to do a reality check on your own beliefs. Following are four examples of erroneous thinking about targets, bullies and bullying.*

"Bullying isn't a problem in my classroom or in our school."

Some teachers and teaching assistants make this claim. In fact:

Bullying in schools is a worldwide problem.... Much of the formal research on bullying has taken place in the Scandinavian countries, Great Britain and Japan, and the problems associated with bullying have been noted and discussed wherever formal schooling environments exist.**

---

* See also 'Expose the Myths' (page 17) and 'Share Facts About Bullying' (pages 18 and 21).
** SOURCE: Ron Banks, 'Bullying in Schools', ERIC Digest EDO-PS-97-17, March 1997.

- The National Association of School Psychologists estimates that 160,000 children miss school every day for fear of being bullied.

"It's best to let children solve their own problems, without adult interference. This is how they learn to get along in the world."

Many adults tell children not to tell tales about bullying. In a normal peer conflict (sharing toys, deciding who goes first in a game, arguing about rules or privileges etc.), children should be allowed and encouraged to figure out and try their own solutions.

Bullying is not a normal peer conflict. Here are two reasons why:

1. In a normal peer conflict, both parties are emotionally involved. Both experience painful or uncomfortable emotions; they're hurt, upset, angry, frustrated, disappointed, outraged etc. In a bullying situation, it's usually only the target who feels emotional pain. In contrast, the bully might feel satisfied, excited or nothing at all (flat affect).

2. In a normal peer conflict, both parties have some power – sometimes equal power, which is why arguments, disagreements and differences of opinion can seem to last forever. In a bullying situation, there's always a power imbalance. The bully has all or most of the power; the target has little or none.

For these reasons, adult intervention with bullying is necessary. This is not 'interference'. It's helping young people with a problem they aren't equipped to solve on their own.

"I've heard that bullying starts in primary school, peaks in the early years of high school and declines towards the end of compulsory education. That sounds almost like 'growing pains'. Maybe bullying is just a normal, unavoidable part of life."

Bullying does seem to follow this very general pattern . . . although many adults experience bullying in their relationships and in the workplace. We get over our 'growing pains', but the effects of being bullied (and of being a bully) can last a lifetime.

For targets, feelings of low self-esteem, isolation, powerlessness and depression can continue into adulthood. The psychological harm they suffer as children can interfere with their social, emotional and academic development. They may develop health problems due to the prolonged stress of being bullied. Some targets drop out of school or college; some commit suicide.

What about bullies? A longitudinal study by psychologist E. Eron at the University of Michigan found that bullies remain bullies throughout their lives. As adults, they have more court convictions, more alcoholism and more personality disorders than the general population. They use more mental health services and have difficulty maintaining relationships.

"I was bullied at school, and I survived. Bullying builds character."

If you were bullied at school, you probably have very clear memories of what happened and how you felt about it. Maybe you even have nightmares related to bullying you experienced as a child. Why would you wish this on any of your pupils? And what kind of "character" does bullying build? If bullying is allowed to continue, children learn that might is right, bullies get their way, aggression is best – and adults can't be counted on to help.

ENCOURAGE A CULTURE OF TELLING

Research has shown that pupils are reluctant to tell adults about bullying. They don't believe it will help; they fear it will make things worse. Often, they're right.

Adults may not act on what they learn. They may not keep the confidence of young people who tell. And if they don't know much about bullying, they may give poor advice – such as "fight back" or "solve your own problems". A tendency not to tell exists, especially as pupils move towards high

school, when the unspoken rule becomes "don't tell on other kids". Meanwhile, bullies make it known that anyone who reports their behaviour will be their next target.

You can and should break this reluctance to report bullying. The 'Creating a Positive Classroom' section of this book describes several ways to do this. *Examples*:

- 'Share Stories About Bullying' (page 24)

- 'Take a Survey' (pages 26 and 33)

- 'Encourage Pupils to Report Bullying and Respond Effectively' (pages 35–36)

- 'Learn More About Your Pupils' (pages 42–43)

- 'Use a Notes-to-the-Teacher Box' (pages 45–46).

As you encourage pupils to come forward with their bullying stories, make sure they know the difference between 'telling on someone' and 'reporting'. Telling on someone is when one pupil tells on another for the purpose of getting the other pupil into trouble. Reporting is when one pupil tells on another for the purpose of protecting someone else. When your pupils fully understand this, reporting will become less of a social taboo and more of a positive, acceptable action.

If a pupil comes to you to report bullying he or she has witnessed:

1. Listen carefully.* Ask questions to clarify the details. Who was involved? What happened? When? Where? Were there any other witnesses? Take notes.

2. If the pupil requests confidentiality, respect his or her wishes.

3. Thank the pupil for talking to you.

If a pupil comes to you to "just talk" and you suspect that he or she is a target of bullying:

1. Be patient. Don't expect all the details to come pouring out immediately. The pupil

---

* See 'Be a Good Listener' (pages 90–92).

may be reluctant to give specifics out of embarrassment or shame.

2. At first, don't question the pupil too closely. Avoid questions that imply he or she might have done something wrong or 'deserved' the bullying in any way.

 Important:
Some targets provoke bullies – by pestering, teasing, fighting back (even though they always lose) and coming back for more. But this doesn't mean they *deserve* to be bullied.

3. Approach the topic gently and indirectly. Give the pupil the option to talk about it or not.

4. If the pupil still skirts the issue, let him or her know that you're willing to listen anytime he or she wants to talk. Leave the door open for future conversations.

5. Once the pupil begins talking about the incident (or several incidents), don't be surprised if it's like a dam breaking. Let the pupil talk. Just listen. Try not to interrupt with suggestions or opinions. This might be the first time the pupil has told anyone about the bullying.

6. Be sympathetic, but don't overreact. The pupil will probably be emotional; it's your job to stay calm. On the other hand, don't trivialise what the pupil tells you. What sounds like simple teasing to you might be terrifying to him or her.

7. Let the pupil know that you believe what he or she is telling you.

8. Ask the pupil whether he or she has any ideas for changing the situation.

 Important:
This boosts self-confidence and self-esteem; you're letting the pupil know that you think he or she is capable of coming up with solutions to the problem. But even if the student has ideas, don't stop here. Bullying is *not* just another peer conflict. It's

always a power imbalance. Adult intervention is required.

9. Ask the pupil whether he or she wants your help. Chances are, the answer will be yes, otherwise the pupil wouldn't have come to you. But sometimes what a target needs most at the moment is an adult who will listen respectfully and believe what he or she says.

10. Offer specific suggestions. (You'll find several throughout this section of the book. See also 'Explore Ways to Deal with Bullies' on pages 45.)

 Important:
If you're not sure what to say or suggest, promise the pupil that you'll get back to him or her. Then seek advice from someone with experience in this area – another teacher, your headteacher or a school counsellor.

11. Redouble your efforts to create a positive classroom where bullying is not tolerated.

12. If at any time the pupil mentions, threatens, or alludes to suicide, take this very seriously. *Get professional help immediately.*

Whether your reporter is a witness or a target, be sure to follow through. Make it very clear that when someone tells you about a bullying incident, you *will* take action and you *won't* just 'let it go'.

ACT IMMEDIATELY

No matter how you're made aware of a bullying incident – whether you witness it personally, a pupil tells you about it, you receive a report in your 'Notes-to-the-Teacher' box (see pages 45–46), you read about it in a pupil's diary (see pages 42–43) or you learn about it in some other way – take immediate action.

IF YOU WITNESS IT PERSONALLY . . .
Intervene there and then. Don't try to talk to anyone involved; don't solicit suggestions on how to resolve the problem. Just put a stop to it.

1. If the bullying is *physical*, say "(Pupil's name), stop (pushing, shoving, hitting, tripping etc.) immediately" in a firm, authoritative voice. Instruct the bully to move away from the target.

If the behaviour has attracted an audience, tell the onlookers to return to their seats, return to their classroom or go somewhere else. When you remove the audience, you remove a large part of the bully's power.

What if the bully and target are fighting? Follow these suggestions from the Crisis Prevention Institute on how to break up a fight:*

- *Get assistance.* Intervening alone is dangerous.

- *Remove the audience.* Onlookers fuel the fire. The intensity of an altercation often parallels the intensity of the bystanders. Remove them as quickly as possible.

- *Avoid stepping between the combatants.* This puts you in a vulnerable position and the combatants' aggression can quickly shift to you.

- *Always try verbal intervention first.* Often one or both combatants are waiting for someone to arrive and stop the fight. Avoid the temptation to immediately revert to physical intervention.

- *Use a distraction.* A distraction (loud noise, flickering of lights etc.) can be enough to break the intensity of the aggression long enough to give you an edge.

- *Separate the combatants.* As soon as possible, break visual contact between the combatants. As long as they can see one another, their hostility is likely to continue.

---

2. If the bullying is *verbal*, say "(Pupil's name), stop (teasing, name-calling, using racist or bigoted remarks etc.) immediately. We don't use those words with each other." Refer to your class rules (see pages 33–34).

3. If the bullying is *emotional*, say "(Pupil's name), stop (intimidating, ignoring, excluding etc.) immediately. In our classroom, everyone is welcome and accepted." Refer to your class acceptance statements (see pages 17–18).

Once you've intervened with the bullying behaviour, your work is just beginning.

WHETHER YOU WITNESS IT PERSONALLY OR LEARN ABOUT IT IN ANOTHER WAY . . .

Consult your school's or local authority's anti-bullying policy on handling bullying incidents. They should include some or all of the following general steps.

 Important:
Keep written records along the way of conversations, actions taken, follow-through etc. You'll want these for reference and also to include in the pupils' files.

1. Talk to the target and the bully *separately* and *soon*. Talk to witnesses one at a time.

For tips on talking to targets, see 'Encourage a Culture of Telling' (pages 87–88). Be sure to offer reassurance that you *will* take action, and you'll do everything in your power to prevent the bullying from happening again.

When talking to bullies, don't ask for their account of what happened. (Bullies generally don't take responsibility for their actions; they deny or minimise their role.) Instead, explain simply and clearly why their behaviour was unacceptable. Refer to school or local authority policies and/or your class rules. Tell them the behaviour you do expect. Spell out the specific consequences of the bullying behaviour as outlined in your school's or local authority's anti-bullying policy, then apply the consequences right away.

Let the bullies know that their parents will be informed.

When talking to witnesses, ask for details. What did they see or hear? Who did what? When? What was the sequence of events? What, if anything, did they (the witnesses) do to stop the bullying? Seek their suggestions for ways to resolve the problem and prevent it from happening again in the future.

2. Talk to other teachers, teaching assistants and staff. Tell them about the bullying incident and also about your conversations with the bully, the target and any witnesses. Seek their advice and insights.

3. Contact the parents or carers of both the bully and the target. If possible, call them that day. Explain what happened, and arrange to meet them at school as soon as schedules allow.

 Important:
You'll want to meet *separately* with each set of parents or carers.

When talking to the target's parents, let them know what happened and what was done to stop it. Explain your school policies and class rules regarding the bullying behaviour, and tell them the consequences. Reassure them that bullying is not tolerated, and that you and the school are taking specific steps to prevent future incidents. Tell them that you will stay in touch with them and let them know how the situation is resolved.

You can share essentially the same information with the bully's parents. Tell them that you'll be working with their child to change his or her behaviour – and you'll need their help.

Depending on the nature and severity of the bullying incident, you may want to have follow-up meetings with the parents to report on the progress being made.

4. Continue to communicate with your colleagues and the parents until the situation is clearly resolved. Monitor the bully's behav-

iour in your classroom; ask other teachers to do the same in the corridors, in the dining hall, in the playground etc. and report back to you on what they see. Tell them that you also want to hear *good* news about the pupil's behaviour, not just bad news. At the same time, monitor the target's safety.

BE A GOOD LISTENER

If a pupil comes to you to report a bullying incident – as a witness or a target – the first and most important thing you should do is *listen*.

It's estimated that we spend about 70 per cent of our waking hours communicating (reading, writing, speaking, listening), and most of that time goes to listening. Yet we receive little or no training on how to listen. In school, we learn how to read, write and speak . . . but not how to listen. We assume that listening 'comes naturally'.

There's an old saying: 'We were born with one mouth and two ears because listening is twice as hard as talking'. Here's how to be a good listener.

DO:
1. **Pay attention and be quiet**. Listening means not talking!

2. **Use attentive body language**. Face the speaker squarely, lean slightly towards him or her and keep your arms and legs uncrossed.

3. **Make and maintain eye contact**. This allows you to pick up on the speaker's body language and facial expressions – important clues to how he or she is feeling.

4. **Be patient**. Allow time for the speaker to say what's on his or her mind. Especially if the speaker is embarrassed or uncomfortable, this might take a while. Also, people generally think faster than they speak. And pupils might not have the vocabulary or life experience needed to find precisely the right words.

5. **Ask for clarification if you need it**. Confirm the accuracy of what you're hearing. *Examples*: "I'm not sure I understand. Could you go over that again?" "Could you repeat that please?" "Can you tell me more about that?"

6. **Empathise**. Try to put yourself in the speaker's place and see his or her point of view.

7. **Ask questions to encourage the speaker and show that you're listening**. *Best*: Open-ended questions. *Worst*: Questions that require simple yes or no answers.

8. **Reflect the speaker's words and feelings from time to time**. *Examples*: "It sounds like you felt hurt when Marcy ignored you at breaktime." "I hear you saying you're angry because of how George treated you." Reflecting (also called mirroring) is simply paraphrasing what the speaker has said – objectively, without interpretation, emotion or embellishment.

9. **Mirror the speaker's feelings in your own face**. If the speaker looks sad, hurt or angry, you should, too.

10. **At points along the way, summarise what you're hearing the speaker say**. Check with the speaker to make sure you've got it right. *Example*: "You're saying that Zach pushed you, and you dropped your books and papers on the floor, and then Zach stepped on your maths book."

11. **Use encouraging body language**. Nod your head, smile, lean a little closer to the speaker (but not too close).

12. **Use brief interjections to indicate that you're listening**. *Examples*: "I see." "Go on." "Tell me more." "Uh-huh." "Really." "Hmmmm." "What then?" "So. . . "

13. **Really concentrate on what the speaker is saying**. Stay focused on his or her words.

14. **Invite the speaker to name his or her feelings**. *Examples*: "When Marcus called you a bad name, how did you feel?" "When Su-Lin made fun of you in front of the others, how did you feel?"

If you listen intently, you should feel somewhat tired afterwards. That's because listening is *active*, not passive.

DON'T:

1. **Talk**. This is not the time to offer your advice or opinions. Wait until *after* the speaker has finished talking or asks for your input.

2. **Interrupt**. You don't like being interrupted when you're talking. Interruptions are rude and disrespectful.

3. **Doodle**. You'll probably want to take notes, however. Tell the speaker why – because you want to keep the facts straight and have a written record of your conversation.

4. **Tap your pen or pencil, shuffle papers, wiggle your foot, look at your watch, yawn etc**. These behaviours indicate boredom.

5. **Argue with, criticise or blame the speaker**. This puts him or her on the defensive.

6. **Mentally argue with the speaker or judge what he or she is saying**. This takes your focus off the speaker's words.

7. **Evaluate or challenge what the speaker is saying**. Just listen.

8. **Interrogate the speaker**. Ask questions for clarification, or to encourage the speaker to tell you more. Make sure your questions don't imply that you doubt what the speaker is saying.

9. **Allow distractions**. Turn off the television, radio, etc. Don't answer the telephone. If someone else approaches you and the speaker, politely but firmly say, "I'm listening to (pupil's name) just now. I'll have time for you when we're finished here."

10. **Think ahead to what you're going to say when the speaker stops talking**. This is called 'rehearsing', and it takes your focus off the speaker.

11. **Let your mind wander**. Sometimes a speaker's words can trigger our own thoughts, memories and associations. If you feel this happening, change your body position and use one of the 'Do's' listed on pages 90–91. This should get you back on track.

12. **Mentally compare what the speaker is saying with what you've heard from other pupils**. If you're gathering information about a bullying incident or series of incidents, take notes and compare your notes later.

Tip: You might share some or all of these do's and don'ts with your pupils. Knowing how to listen is a social skill that builds friendships.

SEND A CLEAR MESSAGE

When you talk to a pupil who has been (or is being) bullied, you may find that the pupil blames himself or herself for being in the wrong place at the wrong time, provoking the bully, doing something to attract the bully's attention or somehow 'asking for it'. Make it very clear that bullying is *never* caused by the target. Tell the pupil:

- It's not your fault that you're being bullied.

- You didn't ask for it.

- You don't deserve it.

- You didn't do anything to cause it.

- Bullying isn't normal. It isn't okay.

- You don't have to face this on your own. I will help you. Other people will help you, too.

You might write these sentences on a card, sign it and give it to the pupil. Or you might ask the pupil to repeat these sentences after you:

- "It's not my fault that I'm being bullied."

- "I didn't ask for it."

- "I don't deserve it."

- "I didn't do anything to cause it."

- "Bullying isn't normal. It isn't okay."

- "I don't have to face this on my own. My teacher will help me. Other people will help me, too."

Strong, positive statements like these can help pupils start feeling better about themselves – a bit more powerful and less like targets.*

PROVIDE COUNSELLING

Being bullied is a very traumatic experience. If at all possible, targets should have access to some type of counselling – by a school psychologist or another trained adult. Peer counselling can also help, if used appropriately.

See whether your school can start a group for victimised pupils or any pupils that you think would benefit from such sessions – a place where they can interact with others, build their social and friendship-making skills and practise getting along. Group meetings can be structured and focus on specific topics (avoiding fights, avoiding bullies, coping with stress, being assertive etc.) or they can be less structured (pupils can talk freely about issues that are important to them).

EMPOWER PARENTS

As you work to make your classroom anti-bullying, get pupils' parents involved and keep them informed. Parents can be your allies – and can also clue you in to bullying situations you might not be aware of.

Tell parents about your efforts to prevent and intervene with bullying in your classroom. You might do this at parent-teacher conferences, on Parents' Evening, during open houses and in notes you send home with pupils.

As early as possible during the school year, give parents copies of 'Helping Children to Combat Bullying' (pages 94–96).

---

* See also 'Teach Pupils to Affirm Themselves' (page 72) and 'Teach Positive Self-Talk' (pages 76–77).

Important:
It's best to give this to parents in person, perhaps as part of a parents'/carers' evening devoted to PSHE issues. If this isn't possible, attach a brief cover letter introducing the handout and explaining why you're sending it home: because you believe *all* parents can benefit from this information. Otherwise you might alarm parents unnecessarily. If 'Helping Children to Combat Bullying' arrives out of the blue, a parent's first thought might be, "Oh no! This must mean that MY child is being bullied!" Preparation and explanation can prevent unnecessary worry and misunderstandings.

MOBILISE BYSTANDERS

According to Denver psychologist (and bullying expert) Carla Garrity, "You can outnumber the bullies if you teach the silent majority to stand up."

Most pupils are neither bullies nor targets. They're witnesses or bystanders – children who might not know what to do and might be afraid to get involved. In some cases, they're the bully's 'lieutenants' or 'henchmen', offering support for the bully and sharing a bit of the bully's power without actually doing the bullying.

In one Canadian study, 43 per cent of pupils said that they try to help the target, 33 per cent said they should help but don't, and 24 per cent said that bullying was none of their business.* If you can 'mobilise the masses' to take action against bullying, you'll significantly reduce the bullying that occurs in your classroom and school.

OFFER SPECIFIC SUGGESTIONS
Pupils can make a difference simply by the way they react when they witness bullying incidents. Share these suggestions with your pupils and ask whether they have ideas of their own.

If you want to stop bullying, you can:

- refuse to join in

- refuse to watch

- speak out ("Don't treat him that way. It's not nice." "Stop hitting her." "Don't use those words." "Don't call him that name." "I'm going to tell the teacher right now.")

- report any bullying you know about or see

- stand up for the person being bullied and gather around him or her, or invite the person to join your group (there's safety in numbers)

- be a friend to the person being bullied

- make an effort to include pupils who are normally left out or rejected

- distract the bully so he or she stops the bullying behaviour.

Explore, possibly through role-play, various ways to react to bullying incidents.

PRAISE BULLY BUSTERS
Encourage pupils to tell you about times when they intervened with bullying incidents or helped put a stop to bullying. Praise them for their courage – because it definitely takes courage to stand up to a bully, especially if you're one of the first to do it.

You could develop an anti-bullying/positive behaviour display board. As part of this display you could include the names of people who stepped in to stop bullying (Bully Busters). You could aim to include everyone's name at some point on this display.

---

* SOURCE: A. Charach, D. Pepler and S. Ziegler, "Bullying at school – a Canadian perspective: A survey of problems and suggestions for intervention", *Education Canada* 35:1 (1995), pp. 12–18.

1. If you think your child is being bullied, *ask your child*. Many children won't volunteer this information; they're ashamed, embarrassed or afraid. Adults need to take the initiative. Ask for specifics and write them down.

    If you suspect that your child won't want to talk about being bullied, try approaching the topic indirectly. You might ask a series of questions like these:

    - "So, who's the bully in your classroom?"

    - "How do you know that person is a bully? What does he or she do?"

    - "What do you think about that?"

    - "Who does the bully pick on most of the time?"

    - "Does the bully ever pick on you?"

    - "What does the bully say or do to you? How does that make you feel?"

2. If your child tells you that he or she is being bullied, *believe your child*. Ask for specifics and write them down.

3. Please DON'T:

    - confront the bully or the bully's parents. This probably won't help and might make things worse.

    - tell your child to "get in there and fight". Bullies are always stronger and more powerful than their targets. Your child could get hurt.

    - blame your child. Bullying is *never* the target's fault.

    - promise to keep the bullying secret. This gives the bully permission to keep bullying. Instead, tell your child you're glad that he or she told you about the bullying. Explain that you're going to help, and you're also going to ask the teacher to help.

4. Contact the teacher as soon as possible. Request a private meeting (no pupils should be around, and ideally no pupils except for your child should know that you're meeting the teacher). Bring your written record of what your child has told you about the bullying, and share this information with the teacher. Ask for the teacher's perspective; he or she probably knows things about the bullying that you don't. Ask to see a copy of the school's anti-bullying policy. Stay calm and be respectful; your child's teacher wants to help.

    Ask what the teacher will do about the bullying. Get specifics. You want the teacher to:

    - put a stop to the bullying

CONTINUED

- have specific consequences for bullying in place, and apply them to the bully

- help the bully change his or her behaviour

- help your child develop bully resistance and assertiveness skills

- monitor your child's safety in the future

- keep you informed of actions taken and progress made.

Important:
It takes time to resolve bullying problems. Try to be patient. The teacher will need to talk to your child, talk to the bully, talk to other children who might have witnessed the bullying and then decide what's best to do for everyone involved.

5. Make a real effort to spend more positive time with your child than you already do. Encourage your child to talk about his or her feelings. Ask your child how the day went. Praise your child as often as possible. Give your child opportunities to do well – by helping you with a chore, taking on new responsibilities or showing off a talent or skill.

6. Help your child develop bully resistance skills. Role-play with your child what to say and do when confronted by a bully. Here are a few starter ideas:

    - Stand up straight, look the bully in the eye, and say in a firm, confident voice, "Leave me alone!" or "Stop that! I don't like that!"

    - Tell a joke or say something silly. (Don't make fun of the bully.)

    - Stay calm and walk away. If possible, walk towards a crowded place or a group of your friends.

    - If you feel you're in real danger, run away as fast as you can.

    - Tell an adult.

    Ask your child's teacher or the school counsellor for more suggestions. Also ask your child for suggestions. It's great if your child comes up with an idea, tries it and it works!

7. Consider helping your child to develop assertiveness skills and more developed relationship skills. If there are local assertiveness training programmes or self-defence classes that children can attend, consider enrolling your child in one. Otherwise, ask your child's school for any advice they have.

Important:
Self-defence classes aren't about being aggressive. They're about avoiding conflict through self-discipline, self-control and improved self-confidence. Most martial arts teach that the first line of defence is non-violence.

CONTINUED

8. If your child seems to lack friends, arrange for him or her to join social groups, clubs or organizations that meet his or her interests. This will boost your child's self-confidence and develop his or her social skills. Confident children with social skills are much less likely to be bullied.

9. Consider whether your child might be doing something that encourages bullies to pick on him or her. Is there a behaviour your child needs to change? Does your child dress or act in ways that might provoke teasing? No one ever *deserves* to be bullied, but sometimes children don't help themselves. Watch how your child interacts with others. Ask your child's teachers for their insights and suggestions.

10. Label everything that belongs to your child with his or her name. Things are less likely to be 'lost' or stolen if they're labelled. Use sew-in labels or permanent marker.

11. Make sure your child knows that his or her safety is always more important than possessions (books, school supplies, toys, money etc.). If your child is threatened by a bully, your child should give up what the bully wants – and tell an adult (you or the teacher) right away.

12. Encourage your child to express his or her feelings around you. Give your child permission to blow off steam, argue, and state opinions and beliefs that are different from yours. If you allow your child to stand up to you now and then, it's more likely that he or she will be able to stand up to a bully.

13. Check with your child often about how things are going. Once your child says that things are better or okay at school – the bullying has slowed down or stopped – you don't have to keep asking every day. Ask once every few days, or once a week. Meanwhile, watch for any changes in behaviour that might indicate the bullying has started again.

14. If you're not already involved with your child's school, get involved. Attend parent-teacher meetings and school meetings. Join the Parent-Teacher Association. Learn about school rules and discipline policies. If you have the time, volunteer to help in your child's classroom or help with school trips.

15. Remember that *you* are your child's most important teacher. Discipline at home should be fair, consistent, age-appropriate and respectful. Parents who can't control their temper are teaching their children that it's okay to yell, scream and use physical violence to get their way.

HAVE STUDENTS SIGN A CLASS PROMISE

Make a copy of the "Class Promise" (page 98). Introduce it by saying that *everyone* can help your classroom become and stay anti-bullying. Read the promise aloud, then pass it around for everyone to sign. Post it in a prominent place in your classroom. Or turn the promise into a large poster and invite pupils to decorate it as well as sign it.

ENCOURAGE A POSITIVE ATTITUDE

All pupils – especially those who have been or are being bullied – can benefit from facing life with a positive attitude. Encourage your pupils to look for what's good in their lives. This might be as simple as a sunrise, warm gloves on a cold day or a puppy's wagging tail. Help them to see that no matter how bad things might seem at the moment, something good is waiting just around the corner.

Use stories of hope and courage to inspire pupils to feel optimistic and reach for the stars. Examples can be found on page 146–151*.

BUILD PUPILS' SELF-ESTEEM

Most bullying targets have low self-esteem. Here are six ways you can build self-esteem in *all* of your pupils.**

STAR CHARTS

Create a separate chart for each pupil. Whenever he or she does something positive or helpful, write it on the chart and decorate it with a star. Or create charts listing specific positive/helpful behaviours you want to encourage in your classroom.

FEEL-GOOD POSTERS

Create a poster for each pupil (or have pupils create their own posters). Put a photograph of the pupil at the centre or ask them to draw a self-portrait. Surround it with positive comments about the pupil. Display the posters in the classroom; they'll be especially noticed and appreciated on Parents' Evening and at open days.

FEEL-GOOD LISTS

Make copies of the handout 'My Feel-Good List' (page 100). Complete the first column for each pupil, then invite pupils to complete the second column. They can share their lists or keep them private – whatever they prefer.

Tip: If any pupils have difficulty completing their columns, offer help. Make simple suggestions. *Examples*: "Everyone has talents, and so do you. What are some of your talents? What are you good at? What do you do best?" They can also take their handouts home and ask their parents and siblings for help.

Tell pupils that whenever they feel down or sad, they can look at their lists and feel better about themselves.

SELF-ESTEEM BOOSTERS

Ask pupils, 'What specific things can you do to feel good about yourself?' Write pupils' ideas on the board. If they have difficulty getting started or run out of ideas too soon, you might suggest some of the following:

- use positive self-talk (see 'Teach Positive Self-Talk', pages 76–77)

- learn a new skill

- develop/strengthen a skill you already have

- start a new hobby

- join a club or group that interests you

- earn money from doing a job

---

* Ask your school librarian or the children's librarian at your local public library to point you towards other appropriate books.
** See also 'Affirm Your Pupils' (pages 71–72), 'Teach Pupils to Affirm Themselves' (page 72), 'Teach Pupils to Affirm Each Other' (pages 72–73 and 76), and 'Teach Positive Self-Talk' (pages 76–77). There are many books and resources available on helping pupils build self-esteem, develop self-confidence, and form a positive self-concept. Several are listed in 'Resources' at the end of this book.

1. We won't bully others.

2. We will help pupils who are being bullied.

3. We will include pupils who are left out.

4. We will report any bullying we know about or see.

Signed:

- volunteer to help someone

- read a book

- get involved in a cause you care about

- take a class in self-defence

- exercise every day

- make a new friend

- be more assertive (see 'Teach Assertiveness Skills', pages 57 and 60)

- get more sleep.

Once you've written a list of ideas on the board, have pupils read it over (or read it aloud to the class) and choose betwee three and five ideas they might like to try. Have them write the ideas in a notebook or on a sheet of paper. Encourage them to try the ideas as soon as possible; offer to help them find resources, get in touch with groups or organisations etc. Wait a few days (or a week), then ask pupils to report on their progress.

CHOICES

Whenever possible, give pupils opportunities to make choices – all kinds of choices. They might decide where to sit, how to arrange their desks, what types of project to work on (written reports, oral reports, art projects etc.). Even if their choices aren't always successful, find something positive about them to recognise. If you must comment on a poor choice (with the goal of helping pupils make better choices next time), do it privately, not publicly.

THEY'RE THE TEACHERS

Set aside time to learn with and from your pupils. Let them tell you about their interests, demonstrate their skills, talents and abilities, and show off a little. Give them opportunities to do things better than you; pupils delight in this, and it gives them a major self-esteem boost.

TEACH POSITIVE VISUALISATION

Let your pupils in on the secret of 'mind over matter'. Arnold Schwarzenegger once said, "As long as you can envisage the fact that you can do something, you can do it – as long as you really believe it 100 per cent."

It's a fact that many successful athletes have improved their performance with positive visualisation – mentally 'seeing' themselves succeed. *Examples*: golfer Jack Nicklaus, champion boxer Muhammad Ali, skier Jean-Claude Killy and tennis stars Billie Jean King and Virginia Wade.

In a famous experiment, an Australian basketball team divided into three groups. All three wanted to be able to shoot more baskets.

- Group 1 practised taking shots for 30 minutes every day. After 20 days, they noticed a 24 per cent improvement.

- Group 2 did nothing. They noticed a 0 per cent improvement.

- Group 3 practised mentally. These players didn't actually shoot baskets. Instead, they imagined themselves shooting baskets. They noticed a 23 per cent improvement – nearly as great as Group 1, who practised for 30 minutes every day.

Learn about positive visualisation and mental imagery. Teach your pupils how to use it – especially those who are or have been targets of bullying or who lack friends, social skills and self-esteem.

Example: Teach pupils to see/imagine themselves getting along with others. With practice, they'll project an attitude of confidence and acceptance, which will improve their chances of fitting in. *Tip*: The more details they can imagine, the better. Can they picture themselves walking into a room? Smiling at people? Saying hello? Can they see people smiling back at them? What do they look like? What are they wearing? What are they saying? How does it feel to be in a group of smiling, welcoming people?

**10 things my teacher
and friends like about me:**

1. _____

2. _____

3. _____

4. _____

5. _____

6. _____

7. _____

8. _____

9. _____

10. _____

**10 things I like
about myself:**

1. _____

2. _____

3. _____

4. _____

5. _____

6. _____

7. _____

8. _____

9. _____

10. _____

PLAY A 'POSITIVE SELF-TALK' GAME

Write a series of put-downs or nasty names on individual slips of paper. Or invite your pupils to do this, but be sure to read the slips before you use them to make sure they're not *too* nasty (or obscene, personal, specific, racist etc.).

Drop the slips into a hat. Invite one pupil to draw a slip out of the hat and give it to you. Write the put-down or name on the board.

Tell the class that they have your permission to call the pupil that name (or use the put-down) *just for now* because you're going to play a game.

Have the class form two lines with enough space between them for you and the pupil to walk comfortably. As you and the pupil walk through the group, the other pupils call him or her the name (or use the put-down). Meanwhile, you whisper positive comments in the pupil's ear. *Examples*: "You're not like that." "You can stay calm." "Don't believe what they say." "You're more mature than they are."

Next, the pupil walks back through the group alone, using positive self-talk ("I'm not like that," "I can stay calm," etc.).

Repeat this game with the other pupils. Afterwards, talk about how they felt when you whispered positive comments to them, and when they used positive self-talk.

For more tips on helping pupils develop this powerful skill, see 'Teach Positive Self-Talk' (pages 76–77).

HELP PUPILS ACCEPT THEIR DIFFERENCES

If you and your pupils did the 'Build Acceptance' activity (pages 17–18), pupils learned ways to accept each other. Targets and potential targets also need to know how to accept themselves.

Most bullying targets are 'different' from the majority in one or more ways. Bullies zero in on differences and make them the focus of their attacks. Children are bullied for being too tall, too short, too thin or too heavy; for having a physical disability or learning difference; for belonging to ethnic, racial, cultural or religious groups that aren't the 'norm'; for having special needs . . . for almost any reason that sets them apart.

How can you help pupils accept themselves? Here are several ideas to try. Ask other teachers and experts (advisory teachers and educational psychologists) for more suggestions.

- Model acceptance and affirmation by learning as much as you can about your pupils' differences. Invite them to educate you.

- When assigning projects and reports, allow pupils to research their differences. A pupil who wears glasses might report on the history of spectacles . . . and identify famous people in history who have worn them. A pupil with a chronic illness might contact a national organisation, learn about other people who have his or her illness and share their stories. Encourage pupils to identify reasons to be proud of their differences and/or positive ways to cope with their differences.

- Help pupils identify role models who share their differences. (*Examples*: Keira Knightley, Jamie Oliver, Albert Einstein, Thomas Edison, Benjamin Zephaniah and racing-car driver Jackie Stewart all have something in common: dyslexia.)

- Ask your librarian or media specialist to recommend books and other resources related to your pupils' differences. Incorporate them into lessons and displays.

- On the Internet, check out Direct Gov, a gateway site to government resources for people with all kinds of disability. Go to: www.disability.gov.uk

- Are there local support groups for people with disabilities and other differences? Find out and get in touch with them. You might invite a speaker to visit your class or school.

- Make it a privilege for pupils to help those with special needs.

- As a class or a school, raise funds to buy a piece of equipment or other resources to help pupils with special needs.

- Help pupils talk more openly about their differences. A willingness to talk indicates a positive attitude and acceptance, which serves as an example for others. Pupils who are embarrassed or ashamed of their differences can become targets for bullies.

- Help pupils develop a sense of humour. Children who can laugh at themselves are better able to cope with teasing. Humour can also defuse potentially volatile situations.

SEE YOUR CLASSROOM THROUGH YOUR PUPILS' EYES

Pupils who are bullied often say that adults "never noticed" the way they were treated. Try seeing your classroom (and yourself) through your pupils' eyes.

Watch how pupils interact. Listen to how they talk to each other. If you were a child, would you be comfortable in your classroom? Would you feel safe, welcome, accepted and free to learn? Is this a place where you could be and do your best without feeling threatened, intimidated or excluded? Would you feel as if the teacher were approachable – as if the teacher would really listen if you reported a problem or asked for help?

Try being a pupil for an hour (or a day). Have your pupils teach the lessons and manage the class. You might learn a great deal about how they see you.

COMBATING BULLYING

Make several copies of 'Ways to Beat Bullying' (page 103). Cut along the dotted lines and give one card to each pupil. (*Tips*: Make copies on heavy paper or thin cardboard. Laminate them for durability.) Spend class time discussing the ideas listed on the cards. Pupils can keep the cards in their pockets or school bags and review them whenever they need ideas or reminders.

Go further:
Get a classroom copy of *Bullies Are a Pain in the Brain*, written and illustrated by Trevor Romain (Free Spirit Publishing, 1997). With wit and humour, this little book teaches children ages 8–13 ways to become bully-proof.

ENCOURAGE STRONG FAMILY RELATIONSHIPS

Do as much as you can to support closeness and togetherness in your pupils' families. *Examples*:

- Work with other teachers and staff to plan open days or evenings, family nights and other events that welcome parents and pupils.

- Bring in speakers who talk about family life and issues.

- Invite pupils to attend parent-teacher conferences with their parents.

- Regularly call or write to parents. Let them know about their children's progress. Report on something special their children did – something that deserves praise and recognition.

- Have pupils interview their parents for homework assignments.

WAYS TO BEAT BULLYING

WAYS TO
BEAT BULLYING

Avoid bullies
Act confident
Look confident
Be observant
Tell a friend
Tell an adult
Be assertive
Stay calm
Keep a safe distance
Walk away
Say "Stop it!"
Say "Leave me alone!"
Say "Whatever!"
Use humour
Use 'I messages'
Travel in a group
Join a group
If you're in danger, RUN

WAYS TO
BEAT BULLYING

Avoid bullies
Act confident
Look confident
Be observant
Tell a friend
Tell an adult
Be assertive
Stay calm
Keep a safe distance
Walk away
Say "Stop it!"
Say "Leave me alone!"
Say "Whatever!"
Use humour
Use 'I messages'
Travel in a group
Join a group
If you're in danger, RUN

WAYS TO
BEAT BULLYING

Avoid bullies
Act confident
Look confident
Be observant
Tell a friend
Tell an adult
Be assertive
Stay calm
Keep a safe distance
Walk away
Say "Stop it!"
Say "Leave me alone!"
Say "Whatever!"
Use humour
Use 'I messages'
Travel in a group
Join a group
If you're in danger, RUN

WAYS TO
BEAT BULLYING

Avoid bullies
Act confident
Look confident
Be observant
Tell a friend
Tell an adult
Be assertive
Stay calm
Keep a safe distance
Walk away
Say "Stop it!"
Say "Leave me alone!"
Say "Whatever!"
Use humour
Use 'I messages'
Travel in a group
Join a group
If you're in danger, RUN

WAYS TO
BEAT BULLYING

Avoid bullies
Act confident
Look confident
Be observant
Tell a friend
Tell an adult
Be assertive
Stay calm
Keep a safe distance
Walk away
Say "Stop it!"
Say "Leave me alone!"
Say "Whatever!"
Use humour
Use 'I messages'
Travel in a group
Join a group
If you're in danger, RUN

WAYS TO
BEAT BULLYING

Avoid bullies
Act confident
Look confident
Be observant
Tell a friend
Tell an adult
Be assertive
Stay calm
Keep a safe distance
Walk away
Say "Stop it!"
Say "Leave me alone!"
Say "Whatever!"
Use humour
Use 'I messages'
Travel in a group
Join a group
If you're in danger, RUN

Start by saying:

> I hear you have been nasty to (pupil's name). Tell me about it.

The bully will probably deny this. Follow up immediately with:

> Yes, but nasty things have been happening to (pupil's name).
> Tell me about it.

Listen to what the bully tells you. Be patient; give him or her time to think, and don't worry about lengthy silences. If the child doesn't respond after a significant period of time has elapsed, say:

> It seems that you don't want to talk today. You'd better go back to class now.

He or she might start talking at this point. If so, just listen. Don't accuse or blame. Avoid asking questions. Try to determine whether the child feels justified in his or her behaviour towards the target. The child might feel quite angry towards the target. Work towards an understanding that the target is having a bad time, whoever is to blame. Say with force and emphasis:

> So, it sounds like (pupil's name) is having a bad time in school.

By now, the child should assent to this. Move on quickly to say:

> Okay. I was wondering what you could do to help (pupil's name) in this situation.

See what solution the child can come up with. Be encouraging. If the child never offers a solution, ask:

> Would you like me to make a suggestion?

If the child offers a solution that depends on someone else's efforts (yours or the target's), say:

> I was thinking about what *you* could do. What could you do?

If the child makes an impractical suggestion, don't reject it. Instead, ask:

> So, if this happened, the bullying would stop?

When the child proposes a practical and relevant solution, say:

> Excellent. You try that out for a week, and we'll meet again and see how you've done. Good-bye for now.

INTERVIEWING A TARGET: SAMPLE SCRIPT

NON-PROVOCATIVE TARGET

Teacher: Hello, Matthew. Sit down. I want to talk to you because I hear some nasty things have been happening to you.

Child: Yes. It's the others in my class. They just keep on picking on me. They won't leave me alone. They mess around with my bag . . . putting stuff in it.

Teacher: You sound as if you're fed up with it.

Child: It just doesn't stop. The rest of the class joins in now.

Teacher: Is there anything you can think of that might help the situation?

Child: I could change schools.

Teacher: Mmm. So you feel it would be better to get out of the situation altogether.

Child: Well, sometimes. But I don't suppose my mother would let me. They're not so bad when I hang around with Simon.

Teacher: So being with someone else helps the situation?

Child: Yes. He backs me up when I tell them to stop it.

Teacher: So he supports you?

Child: Yes. I could sit next to him.

Teacher: Okay. You do that over the next week and then we'll have another chat to see how things have been going. Okay? Goodbye.

PROVOCATIVE TARGET

Teacher: Hello, Matthew. Sit down. I want to talk to you because I hear some nasty things have been happening to you.

Child: Yes. It's the others in my class. They just keep on picking on me. They won't leave me alone. They mess around with my bag . . . putting stuff in it.

Teacher: You sound as if you're fed up with it.

Child: It just doesn't stop. The rest of the class joins in now.

Teacher: Tell me more about what happens. How does it all start?

Child: It's usually when I go over and sit by them. They just can't take a joke.

Teacher: So you play jokes on them?

Child: Yes, just messing around. I go on really good holidays and they never do so I ask them where they are going . . . it makes them really mad. They're just jealous.

Teacher: Then they get angry with you. What happens when they get angry with you?

Child: Well, that's when they started messing around with my bag.

Teacher: Is there anything you can think of that might help the situation?

Child: I guess I could leave them alone.

Teacher: Okay. You do that over the next week and then we'll have another chat to see how things have been going. Okay? Goodbye.

ENCOURAGE RELATIONSHIPS WITH OTHER ADULTS

When pupils develop close relationships with adults – not only their parents, but also other family and community members – they learn important social skills and build their self-confidence and self-esteem. This is important for *all* pupils, and can be especially beneficial to those who lack social skills and are targets or potential targets of bullying.

SCHOOL STAFF

Do teachers, teaching assistants and other staff members make the effort to get to know pupils? Do they run clubs, coach teams, supervise before-school and after-school activities, lead discussion groups for children and/or run a shool council? Do they take time to listen to pupils' concerns and offer support and advice? Talk to your colleagues. What can you do individually and together to form positive, meaningful relationships with pupils?

Enlist the help of all school staff in making pupils feel welcome, accepted and appreciated. TAs, MSAs, school cooks, librarians, office personnel and others can greet pupils by name, share a kind word with them and intervene if they see a pupil being mistreated.

Encourage school staff to find ways for pupils with low self-esteem or poor social skills to shine. *Examples*: A pupil could deliver the headteacher's telephone messages or help younger children do library research.

GRANDPARENTS

Encourage pupils to spend time with their grandparents, sharing their problems and concerns as well as their achievements.

Because many of your pupils might not be in regular contact with their grandparents, consider establishing an Adopt-a-Grandparent programme in cooperation with a retirement home.

Arrange for your class to visit their adopted grandparents regularly. Take class plays, presentations and musical performances to them. Make artwork for the grandparents' rooms and send them cards on special occasions. Invite all grandparents to visit your pupils at school and volunteer in your classroom and on school trips.

CLUBS, GROUPS AND TEAMS

Create a directory of local organisations and clubs that you think pupils might be interested in. This directory could include Guide, Brownie, Cub and Scout groups, sports clubs and teams, drama clubs, dance clubs, youth clubs, music groups and choirs and anything else of interest. Ask pupils to tell you about anything they are currently or have been involved in so you can add to your directory. You might also ask pupils to talk about the activities they have done as a result of the groups they belong to.

You might also invite representatives to visit your class, talk about their organisations and talk to your pupils.

MENTORS

Children of all ages have formed strong relationships with mentors – caring adults who make active, positive contributions to their lives. You might find out whether teachers, teaching assistants and other school staff are willing to serve as mentors; match them up with pupils who share their interests and arrange for them to spend time together. Parents might be available to mentor other pupils in your class.

PROVIDE SAFE HAVENS

Pupils who are bullied at school need places to go where they feel safe and accepted. Work with other teachers, your headteacher and staff to set aside a special room or place where all pupils are welcome. Provide adequate supervision. Older pupils can help run a quiet activities room.

If space in your school is tight, you might identify a corner of the dining hall or library as a safe haven. Or use your classroom Peace Place (see page 64).

PLAY "WHAT IF?"

Lead class discussions, small group discussions or role-plays around "What If?" questions. *Examples*:

- What if you're walking down the corridor and someone calls you a bad name?

- What if someone tries to make you give him (or her) your lunch money?

- What if someone picks a fight with you?

- What if someone pushes you down in the playground?

- What if someone spreads a nasty rumour about you?

Invite pupils to contribute their own "What If?" questions to talk about or act out. Don't be surprised if this takes an interesting twist. The questions pupils offer might relate to real bullying incidents they have experienced or witnessed – and that you haven't heard about until now.

As pupils come up with suggestions or role-play possible ways of coping with problem situations, remind them that bullies enjoy having control over their targets. They target individuals who cannot defend themselves and lack confidence. Guide pupils to come up with answers that are assertive, confident and strong – and, at the same time, aren't likely to make things worse.

Tip: If you and your pupils haven't done the 'Explore Ways to Deal with Bullies' activity (page 45), you might want to do this before playing "What If?"

EQUALISE THE POWER

Bully–target relationships always involve the unequal distribution of power. Bullies have it, targets don't – or bullies have most of it and targets have very little.

Look for opportunities to boost the power of pupils who are bullied or at risk of being bullied. *Examples*:

- Praise them sincerely, appropriately and publicly.

- Learn their skills and areas of expertise, then suggest that other pupils consult them as 'experts' on a topic.

- Show that you trust them and have confidence in their abilities. From time to time, give them special tasks to do. Make sure these are tasks that other pupils would find desirable and enjoyable. Assigning jobs no one really wants to do further stigmatises targets and potential targets.

Equalising the power can be a delicate balance. You'll want to offer targets chances to succeed – but without making them 'teacher's pets'. (See also 'Give Them Opportunities to Shine', page 108). Be careful not to pit targets and bullies against each other as you're handing out praise and special tasks. This might make the bully even more determined to show the target who's in charge.

GET PUPILS INVOLVED IN GROUPS

Pupils who are bullied have plenty of experience feeling isolated, excluded, rejected and afraid. They need experience feeling welcome, safe and accepted.

You might start a counselling group (see 'Provide Counselling', page 92) for *any* pupils who need help making friends and practising social skills – not just bullying targets. Other types of group to consider are:

- a peer support group

- a new pupil orientation group

- a cooperative learning group

- a special interest group or club.

For pupils who aren't ready to integrate with their peers during unstructured times (such as break-time), you might start a club that meets at those times. This approach has been used effectively in some schools. Meetings can be structured around specific topics (how to make friends, how to stand up to bullies etc.), or pupils can learn and practise social skills. Some of the meetings should be set aside for fun and play.

This club also provides an alternative for pupils who are new to the school and not yet comfortable or confident in the playground. The club should provide a well-supervised environment that allows and encourages friendships to form. Once they do, pupils may be less reluctant to go outside and play.

You can also suggest that pupils get involved with groups and clubs. Parents can also arrange these opportunities for their children; you might raise the topic during a parent-teacher conference. The goals of any group involvement should be to develop the pupil's peer support network, self-confidence and social skills.

GIVE THEM OPPORTUNITIES TO SHINE

Increase pupils' social contacts by giving them specific responsibilities that are social in nature. *Examples*: tutoring other pupils on the computer, working in the school office, mentoring younger pupils, reading aloud to younger pupils, being in charge of group projects. This offers them opportunities to interact with others, help their peers and demonstrate their skills. Plus assigning pupils these responsibilities shows that you trust and accept them. (See also 'Equalise the Power', page 107.)

Help pupils discover and develop their talents and skills. This boosts their self-confidence and increases their standing among their peers. *Example*: If one of your pupils enjoys making kites, he or she could bring some examples for show-and-tell, teach other pupils what he or she knows, and lead a project on kite-making related to a science or geography lesson.

ASK PUPILS TO KEEP DIARIES

Writing is a way to get in touch with our feelings, record events in our lives, formalise our plans and goals and explore what's important to us. For pupils who are bullied, writing is a way to regain some of the power they've lost – and keep track of important details (what happened when, who did or said what) that you and other adults can use to stop the bullying and prevent future bullying. Written records make bullying easier to prove.

If possible, give pupils spiral-bound notebooks.* In one-on-one or small group meetings, explain or demonstrate some of the ways they might use their diaries. Or give them a topic to write about each week. *Examples*:

- a time when I was bullied (what happened, who was there, how I felt about it, what I did about it)

- a list of people I can talk to about my problems – people I trust

- a list of people I can count on to help me

- a list of things I can say when a bully teases me or calls me names

- a list of funny things I can say to a bully

- ways to build my self-esteem

- good things I can tell myself (positive self-talk).

Pupils might use their diaries to tell you about things that are happening in their lives – things they don't feel comfortable talking about.

TEACH PLANNING SKILLS

Pupils can learn to dodge potential bullying situations by planning ahead. With the whole class or in small groups, work with pupils to brainstorm ways to avoid bullies, ways to stay safe in their everyday lives and ways to be more observant. *Examples*:

_____

* See also 'Weekly Diary' (pages 42–43).

- When you're walking down the corridor and you see a bully, don't make eye contact. Stay as far away from the bully as you can. Try to keep other people between you. If possible, turn and go in a different direction.

- Travel in groups. When you're in the playground, stay close to a friend or two. When you're in the dining hall, sit with children who are friendly to you.

- Make a list of places where you feel unsafe. Plan to stay away from those places. If that's not possible, make sure you never go to those places alone. This might mean changing your route to school, avoiding parts of the playground or only using rooms that always have other people in them.

- If you notice a bully coming towards you, walk calmly but quickly in the opposite direction.

- Stay away from anyone who makes you feel uncomfortable, anxious, scared, worried or nervous.

- When you're walking in a public place, don't look at the ground. Look around you and notice who else is there.

- Always let a trusted friend or caring adult know where you're going.

- Stick with a group, even if they aren't your friends.

Distribute copies of 'Planning Ahead' (page 112). Pupils can complete them on their own, or work in pairs or small groups. Afterwards, share and discuss responses. Praise pupils for coming up with good ideas.

TEACH POWER SKILLS

Teach these skills to pupils you believe are ready to go beyond the basics (stay calm, walk away, join a group, tell an adult). Use demonstration, discussion, role-playing and plenty of guided practice. *Note*: Some pupils may be too timid to try these approaches. If that's the case, don't force it.

1. Agree with everything the bully says

Examples: "Yes, that's true." "You're right." "I see what you mean." "You are absolutely 100 per cent correct! I am a wimp!"

2. Disarm the bully with humour

Laugh and walk away. Or laugh and don't walk away. Act as if the two of you are sharing a good joke. Play along. When the bully starts laughing, you can say something like, "Wow, that was fun! See you later. Gotta go!"

Turn a put-down into a joke. *Example*: "You called me a wimp. You're right; I need to lift weights more often."

3. Bore the bully with questions

Examples: "I'm a wimp? What do you mean by that? How do you know I'm a wimp? Do you know any other wimps? Have you compared me to them? Am I more or less wimpy than they are? What exactly is a wimp, anyway?"

4. Be a broken record

Whatever the bully says, say the same thing in response... over and over and over again. Examples:

Bully: "You're a wimp."

You: "That's your opinion."

Bully: "Yeah, and I'm right."

You: "That's your opinion."

Bully: "So what are you going to do about it?"

You: "That's your opinion."

Bully: "You'd better shut up."

You: "That's your opinion."

Bully: "I'm getting sick of you."

You: "That's your opinion."

Bully: "I mean it! Shut up!"

You: "That's your opinion."

Bully: "Oh, forget it!"

Bully: "You want to fight?"

You: "I don't do that."

Bully: "That's because you're a wimp."

You: "I don't do that."

Bully: "You're too scared to fight. You're chicken."

You: "I don't do that."

Bully: "I'll bet I can make you fight."

You: "I don't do that."

Bully: "What's with you? Is that all you can say?"

You: "I don't do that."

Bully: "Oh, forget it!"

5. Just say no

Examples: "You can't have this toy. I'm playing with it now." "You can't have my lunch. I'm eating it." "You can't have my money. I need it to buy lunch later." "You can't have my pencil. I need it. Give it back."

6. Use 'fogging'

If being assertive and telling a bully to stop calling you names doesn't work, try responding with short, bland words and phrases that neutralise the situation. *Examples*: "Possibly." "You might be right." "It might look that way to you." "Maybe." "That's your opinion."

7. Exhaust the topic*

Stay calm and confident. Respond to the bully by asking questions after each put-down that require the bully to explain or expand on his or her comments. *Example*: "You called me 'fatso.' What do you mean by 'fatso'? Can you explain how big a person has to be in order to be fat? How many pupils in our school are fat?" The bully may get tired of the questioning and walk away.

---

*Reprinted from *Childhood Bullying and Teasing* by Dorothea M. Ross, PhD (Alexandria, VA: American Counseling Association, 1996), © ACA. Reprinted with permission. No further reproduction authorised without written permission of the American Counseling Association.

8. Make an asset of the topic*

If a bully targets a difference and uses it as a topic for put-downs, turn the difference into an asset. *Example*: A pupil lost his hair after a series of medical treatments. A bully started teasing him about it. The pupil explained that a lot of famous people are bald, and he hoped he'd stay bald at least until Halloween. This took the bully by surprise, and he stopped the teasing.

9. Make the bully look ignorant about medical conditions*

Correct the bully by giving accurate information about your medical condition. Then say something like, "You must not read much, or you'd know that."

PROTECT YOURSELF

Teachers can be bullied, too. Maybe you have an intimidating or aggressive parent – someone who makes you feel uneasy or threatened. Or maybe the problem is a colleague, a group of your colleagues or a superior.

1. What if you're being bullied by your colleagues or superiors?

(Workplace bullying is on the rise, and schools are workplaces, just like businesses or factories.) Talk to your headteacher. Talk to your union representative. You don't have to put up with rude, hostile behaviour or put-downs. Learn about the laws that protect you.

Go further
There is plenty of guidance and advice on the Internet about how to deal with bullying in the workplace. One example is http://www.direct.gov.uk/en/Employment/Employees/DiscriminationAtWork/DG_10026670.
However, every local authority should have an anti-bullying policy that clearly outlines what an individual needs to do if they are being bullied in the workplace. It should be straightforward to order a copy.

2. **Meanwhile, here are some common-sense tips you can follow to safeguard yourself:**

    • Vary your routine. If you walk to and from school, don't always walk the same route at the same time. If you drive, change your route frequently (and try stopping for coffee at a different place now and then).

    • Pay attention to your intuition; act on it. It's better to be safe and risk a little embarrassment than stay in an uncomfortable situation that may turn out to be dangerous.

    • Don't label keys with your name or any identification.

    • Try not to overload yourself with books and other materials when walking to and from the school building.

    • Before or after school hours, check your surroundings before getting out of your car.

    • Have your keys ready before you leave the school building. Look inside and under your car before getting in, and always lock your car.

    • If your school has a lift, stay close to the controls and locate the emergency button.

    • Get to know your colleagues and look out for each other.

    • Walk with confidence. Be assertive. Watch your body language. (See pages 57 and 60.)

    • Be extra watchful when you're walking between buildings, in poorly lighted areas etc. Try to have another adult with you.

    • If you feel that you're in serious, immediate danger from a bully, don't try to defuse the situation on your own. Get help from school security or police officers.

PLANNING AHEAD

Ways to avoid bullies:

Ways to stay safe:

Ways to be observant:

Bullies need help – the sooner the better. Bullying among primary school-age children is recognised as an antecedent to more violent behaviour when they get older. If children don't learn to change their behaviours, bullying becomes a habit that carries forward into their teens and their lives as adults.

Although bullies may be popular in primary school (because they're powerful, others look up to them), their popularity wanes during late adolescence; by the time they reach high school, their peer group may be limited to other bullies. They may get into trouble with the law; studies show that one in four bullies will have a criminal record before age 30. They may bully their spouses, children and colleagues and have difficulty forming and sustaining healthy, positive relationships.

The 'Creating a Positive Classroom' section of this book includes many tips and strategies that can help all pupils – including bullies – learn better ways of relating to others. Some of the strategies in 'Helping Targets' can be adapted for use with bullies and potential bullies. *Examples*:

- 'Encourage a Positive Attitude' (page 97).

- 'Build Pupils' Self-Esteem' (pages 97 and 99); although it's a myth that all bullies have low self-esteem, some do.

- 'Teach Positive Visualisation' (page 99).

- 'Give Them Opportunities to Shine' (page 108).

Some of the strategies in 'Helping Targets' will benefit all of your pupils. *Examples*:

- 'Encourage Strong Family Relationships' (page 102).

- 'Encourage Relationships with Other Adults' (page 106).

'Helping Bullies' focuses mainly on suggestions for working with bullies or potential bullies. As you try these ideas in your classroom, here are some good things you can expect to happen:

Your pupils will learn how to:

- change their thinking
- know what to expect when they use inappropriate behaviour
- accept responsibility for their behaviour
- manage their anger
- explore positive ways to feel powerful
- understand why they bully others
- stop bullying.

You'll discover how to:

- identify bullies or potential bullies
- have clear consequences in place
- work to change bullies' behaviour – without being a bully yourself
- communicate with parents
- teach pupils positive ways to feel powerful
- change bullies' thinking, not just their behaviour.

 Important:

Most children can change their behaviour with guidance and help from caring adults. Sometimes, however, you might encounter a pupil who resists your efforts and simply won't change. Find out ahead of time what your school and local authority are prepared to do in these extreme circumstances. When you truly run out of options – when strategies don't work, the parents can't or won't support your efforts, and the pupil's behaviour gets progressively worse – you may have no choice but to take the problem to your headteacher and leave it in their hands. The ideas in this book are not intended to help incorrigible bullies or children with severe behavioural and personality problems.

CATCH THEM IN THE ACT

The first and most important thing you can do to help bullies is notice their behaviour and respond appropriately.

Obviously, you want to catch them 'being bad' – teasing, using hurtful words, intimidating other pupils, hitting, shoving, kicking and so on – and put a stop to that behaviour as soon as you become aware of it. See 'Act Immediately' (pages 88–90) for specific suggestions on intervening with bullying you witness personally or learn about in another way; see also 'Have Clear Consequences in Place' (pages 123–125).

Not as obviously (and sometimes not as easily), you also want to *catch them being good*. No one can be a bully 24 hours a day; even the worst bully takes an occasional break. Bullies need 'praise' as much as other pupils – probably more.

- Recognise and reward positive and accepting behaviours whenever you observe them. This will increase the likelihood that such behaviours will be repeated.

- Go the extra distance and praise behaviours you might take for granted in other pupils – waiting one's turn, sharing, saying please or thank you.

- Create situations that give bullies the opportunity to shine. *Examples*: Ask a problem pupil to help you with an important project. Or send an older bully to a younger class to help a pupil practise spelling words or do maths problems. Then recognise your pupil's positive behaviour.

Of course, you'll want to notice and praise positive, sociable behaviours in *all* of your pupils. You can do this verbally each day ("Thanks for helping, Evan." "Nice job, class. You're making our new pupil feel welcome."). You might also award special certificates recognising specific behaviours. Pupils will appreciate Reward Certificates (page 116) – and parents will treasure them.

Tip: In one school, pupils who are seen or reported as displaying positive social interactions (sticking up for a friend, making a new friend, welcoming or accepting a new pupil, being a good role model, cooperating, showing empathy etc.) are given a 'Gotcha!' card to sign. The cards are entered in a prize draw at the end of each week.

 Go further:
Work with other teachers and teaching assistants to arrange a special celebratory awards assembly to be held once a month or several times a year. Try to schedule it for a time when parents and grandparents can attend. Instead of handing out the usual awards – for athletic or academic achievement – reserve this assembly for pupils whose sociable behaviours have made a positive difference in your classroom and school.

Finally: monitor your own interactions with your pupils. Are they mostly negative, mostly positive or a mixture of both? Make an effort to increase the number of positives – smiles, acknowledgments, words of praise and approval, thank-yous, nods. The National Association of School Psychologists (NASP) recommends that teachers give approximately *five positives* for each negative. Keep track of your behaviour for a day or two. How close do you come to the five-to-one ratio? Is there room for improvement?

HAVE COMPASSION

Bullies can be distracting, disruptive, annoying, frustrating and even scary at times. But they need as much help, understanding and compassion as you can give them. Food for thought:

- Many bullies have family problems – parents, siblings or other bigger, stronger people who bully them. They don't know other ways to behave. And even if they learn and observe other ways in your classroom, they experi-

ence a sort of 'dissonance' when they return home. Like children of divorced parents who alternate between their parents' homes, they must fit into both environments, and it's not easy.

- Many bullies are angry all or most of the time. Being angry is no fun – especially if you're not really sure *why* you're angry, you don't have anyone to talk to about your anger (or think you don't, and even if you do, you might not know *how* to talk about it) and your peers avoid and fear you. For some bullies, being angry is a vicious circle, and they're caught in the middle with no way out.

- It's hard to be the meanest, toughest child in the classroom or in the playground. You're always having to prove yourself and fend off other children who want to take over as meanest and toughest.

- It's hard to feel that you always have to win and can't ever lose. No one likes to lose, but bullies can't afford to lose – it's too risky. So they cheat, play dirty and intimidate anyone who stands in their way. And eventually no one wants to play with them or against them.

- Many bullies are jealous of other people's success. Jealousy is a nasty, uncomfortable feeling. It's so overpowering that it can prevent you from enjoying your own successes – or distract you so much that you don't achieve your true potential.

- Some bullies never wanted to hurt or harass anyone else. They were bullied by someone else into joining a bully gang and are going along just to stay on the bully's good side.

- Bullies lack social skills. When you don't know how to get along with others, and when you see groups of friends hanging out, laughing, telling jokes and enjoying each other's company, you know you're missing out on something important . . . but you don't know how to get it for yourself. Which may be another reason why bullies are so angry.

- Bullies have hangers-on, 'henchmen', or 'lieutenants', but they seldom have real friends. Life without friends is lonely.

Brilliant **Wonderful** Congratulations

Fantastic stuff!!!
Super

Today's date: _____

Your name: _____

You have been awarded this certificate because:

Teacher's signature: _____

The bullies in your classroom may be some of the most unpleasant, least appealing children you know. The good news is, they're still children . . . for now. As children, they have the potential to learn, grow and change.

IDENTIFY BULLIES OR POTENTIAL BULLIES

You may know that some pupils in your classroom are bullies; either you've seen them in action yourself, or you've heard reports from other pupils and teachers. But what about the bullies whose actions aren't noticed by adults, whose targets are too intimidated or ashamed to come forward, and whose witnesses either don't want to get involved or fear reprisals if they do? And what about those pupils who haven't started bullying others but may be heading in that direction?

'Identify Targets or Potential Targets' (pages 82–85) explains how to look for warning signs and seek input from pupils' parents. You can use similar approaches to identify bullies or potential bullies.

LOOK FOR WARNING SIGNS

For any pupil you suspect might be a bully or potential bully, complete the 'Warning Signs' checklist (pages 118–119).

Important:
These forms should be kept confidential. You may want to share them with other adults – teachers, your headteacher, the school counsellor, the pupil's parents – but they should never be accessible to pupils.

GET PARENTS' INPUT

If a pupil shows some or many of the warning signs, contact the parents. Arrange a face-to-face meeting at school. You may want to include the special educational needs coordinator (SENCO) or behavioural psychologist in the meeting.

No parent wants to hear that his or her child might be a bully or potential bully, so you'll need to han-

dle this *very* carefully. You might start by emphasising your commitment to creating a positive classroom environment where every pupil is valued, accepted, safe and free to learn. Share information about what's being done at your school to reduce bullying.

Next, tell the parents about the *positive* behaviours you've observed in their child. (See 'Catch Them in the Act', pages 114–115.) Parents love hearing good things about their children, and this sets the stage for a productive meeting.

Then tell the parents that you've noticed some behaviours at school which may indicate their child is bullying others or might be headed in that direction. Give examples. Explain that there are other behaviours that don't show up at school, and you need their help identifying those behaviours.

Ask if they have noticed any of the following in their child:

- having more money than he or she can explain

- buying things he or she normally can't afford

- having new possessions (games, clothing, CDs etc.) and claiming that "my friends gave them to me"

- defying parental authority; ignoring or breaking rules; pushing parental boundaries harder than ever

- behaving aggressively towards siblings

- exhibiting a sense of superiority – of being 'right' all the time

- being determined to win at everything; being a poor loser

- blaming others for his or her problems

- refusing to take responsibility for his or her negative behaviours.

What else can the parents tell you? What else have they noticed that you should know – that might help you help their child?

WARNING SIGNS - WHAT TO LOOK FOR

The following behaviours and traits may indicate that a pupil is bullying others or, if bullying isn't yet evident or hasn't been reported, has the potential to become a bully. For any pupil you're concerned about, tick all that apply.

_____ 1. Enjoys feeling powerful and in control.

_____ 2. Seeks to dominate and/or manipulate peers.

_____ 3. May be popular with other pupils, who envy his or her power.

_____ 4. Is physically larger and stronger than his or her peers.

_____ 5. Is impulsive.

_____ 6. Loves to win at everything; hates to lose at anything. Is both a poor winner (boastful, arrogant) and a poor loser.

_____ 7. Seems to derive satisfaction or pleasure from others' fear, discomfort or pain.

_____ 8. Seems overly concerned with others 'disrespecting' him or her; equates 'respect' with fear.

_____ 9. Seems to have little or no empathy for others.

_____ 10. Seems to have little or no compassion for others.

_____ 11. Seems unable or unwilling to see things from another person's perspective or 'walk in someone else's shoes'.

_____ 12. Seems willing to use and abuse other people to get what he or she wants.

_____ 13. Defends his or her negative actions by insisting that others "deserved it", "asked for it", or "provoked" him or her; a conflict is always someone else's "fault".

_____ 14. Is good at hiding negative behaviours or doing them where adults can't notice.

_____ 15. Gets excited when conflicts arise between others.

_____ 16. Stays cool during conflicts in which he or she is directly involved.

_____ 17. Exhibits little or no emotion (flat affect) when talking about his or her part in a conflict.

CONTINUED →

_____ **18**. Blames other people for his or her problems.

_____ **19**. Refuses to accept responsibility for his or her negative behaviours.

_____ **20**. Shows little or no remorse for his or her negative behaviours.

_____ **21**. Lies in an attempt to stay out of trouble.

_____ **22**. Expects to be 'misunderstood', 'disrespected' and picked on; attacks before he or she can be attacked.

_____ **23**. Interprets ambiguous or innocent acts as purposeful and hostile; uses these as excuses to strike out at others verbally or physically.

_____ **24**. 'Tests' your authority by committing minor infractions, then waits to see what you'll do about it.

_____ **25**. Disregards or breaks school and/or class rules.

_____ **26**. Is generally defiant or oppositional towards adults.

_____ **27**. Seeks/craves attention; seems just as satisfied with negative attention as positive attention.

_____ **28**. Attracts more than the usual amount of negative attention from others; is shouted at or disciplined more often than other pupils.

_____ **29**. Is street-wise.

_____ **30**. Has a strong sense of self-esteem. _Tip_: This is contrary to the prevailing myth that bullies have low self-esteem. In fact, there's little evidence to support the belief that bullies victimise others because they feel bad about themselves.

_____ **31**. Seems mainly concerned with his or her own pleasure and well-being.

_____ **32**. Seems antisocial or lacks social skills.

_____ **33**. Has difficulty fitting into groups.

_____ **34**. Has a close network of a few friends (actually 'henchmen' or 'lieutenants'), who follow along with whatever he or she wants to do.

_____ **35**. May have problems at school or at home; lacks coping skills.

Important:
Studies show that bullies often come from homes where physical punishment is used, where children are taught to handle problems by striking back physically, and where parental involvement and warmth are minimal or lacking. But never *assume* that this is true for every child. In my experience, parents of bullies are deeply concerned about their children. They want their children to be accepted by others; they want them to develop social skills, friendships, and positive character traits including tolerance, compassion and empathy. So instead of expecting the worst, hope for the best. Project a sense of optimism; communicate your belief that you and the parents can work together to turn the child around.

You'll also want to talk to the parents about how bullying breaks your school and classroom policies and rules. Mention the consequences of such behaviour, but don't dwell on these too long. Rather, the purpose of this meeting should be to identify warning signs and reach an agreement that everyone involved – you, the parents and the SENCO (if present) – will work together to help the pupil. Make it clear that you have high expectations that the problem can and will be resolved successfully. You want the parents to leave your meeting with a desire to work with you on their child's behalf, not the feeling that you and the school are united 'against' them and their child.

Towards the end of the meeting, give parents a copy of 'Bringing Out the Best in Children: Tips for Parents' (pages 121–122). Explain that this is a list of suggestions they can try at home. Answer any questions they may have. *Tip*: You may want to find out ahead of time about parenting courses and resources available in your locality, so you can give this information to parents who want it.

Thank the parents for coming in and talking to you. Tell them that you'll communicate with them often about their child's behaviour and progress, and ask them to do the same for you. Then be sure to follow through.

Make a written record of your meeting. Note any relevant information the parents shared with you, any conclusions you came to and any agreements you reached.

NEVER BULLY THE BULLY

When faced with a bully and frustrated or angered by his or her behaviour, it's easy for adults to 'lose their cool'. Shouting and threats aren't uncommon.

Severe punishment may suppress the current behaviour, but it doesn't teach alternative behaviours, including positive ways to act. Here are eight more reasons why 'bullying the bully' is always a bad idea:

1. Adults who respond to bullies with violence, force or intimidation are modelling and reinforcing the same behaviours they're trying to change. Children imitate what they see adults do.

2. Severe punishment reinforces the power imbalance and shows children that bullying is acceptable.

3. Severe punishment may stop one behaviour temporarily but stimulate other aggressive behaviours.

4. The child may stop the punished behaviour only when adults are around and increase it in other settings.

5. The child may strike back at the adult who's doing the punishing, or strike out at someone else because of displaced anger.

6. Angry children who don't fear authority may become even angrier and focus on getting revenge.

7. Frequent punishment may cause some children to withdraw, regress and give up. Others may feel a strong sense of shame and low self-esteem.

8. Severe punishment is a short-term 'solution' that may cause more problems down the road. ("If adults can hit, why can't I? Maybe I just have to wait until I'm bigger.")

1. Have regular home meetings with your child. Show interest in what he or she is doing. Ask questions and be a good listener. Who are your child's friends? What are your child's likes and dislikes? How does your child spend his or her time at school, and away from school when he or she isn't with the family? *Tip*: Some of the best family discussions happen around the dinner table.

2. Make a real effort to spend more positive time with your child than you already do. Try to do things together that your child enjoys. Encourage your child to talk about his or her feelings. Ask how the day went. Praise your child as often as possible. Give your child opportunities to do well – by helping you with a chore, taking on new responsibilities or showing off a talent or skill.

3. Monitor the television shows your child watches, and reduce the amount of TV violence he or she is exposed to. Experts have found that TV violence has a negative effect on children. Also limit the amount of violence your child encounters in video and computer games.

4. Supervise your child's whereabouts and activities even more closely than you already do. Set reasonable rules and limits for activities and curfews. Make it a point to always know where your child is and who he or she is with.

5. Consider helping your child to develop skills in conflict resolution, stress and anger management and more developed relationship skills. If there are relevant local training programmes or self-defence classes that children can attend, consider enrolling your child in one. Otherwise, ask your child's school for any advice they might be able to give to support you in addressing these issues.

 Important:
Self-defence classes aren't about being aggressive. They're about avoiding conflict through self-discipline, self-control, and improved self-confidence. Most martial arts teach that the first line of defence is non-violence.

6. If your child's teacher has told you that your child is bullying others, take it seriously. Children who bully often have serious problems later in life.

   • Talk to your child. Be aware that your child might deny or minimise his or her behaviour; this is normal. Don't blame; don't ask "why" something happened or "why" your child acted in a certain way, because this may lead to lies and excuses. Stay calm and make it clear that bullying is NOT okay with you.

   • Reassure your child that you still love him or her. It's the bullying *behaviour* you don't like. Tell your child that you'll work together to help change the behaviour – and you won't give up on him or her.

→ *CONTINUED*

- Talk to your child's teacher(s) and other adults at the school – in private, when no other pupils are around. Get the facts on your child's behaviour. Ask them to keep you informed.

- Work with the school to modify your child's behaviour. Stay in touch with teachers, teaching assistants and playground supervisors so you know how your child is progressing. Let them know about your efforts at home.

- Apply reasonable, age-appropriate, developmentally appropriate consequences (withdrawing privileges, giving time-outs, assigning extra jobs around the house) for bullying behaviour. Avoid corporal punishment, which sends your child the message that 'might is right'.

- Talk to your child about how bullying affects the target. If you remember times from your own childhood when you were bullied, you know how much it hurts.

- Help your child learn and practise positive ways to handle anger, frustration and disappointment. (How do you handle those feelings at home? Remember: you're an important role model for your child.) Try role-playing new behaviours with your child.

- Praise your child's efforts to change. Praise your child for following home and school rules. The more positives you can give your child, the better. *Tip*: Try giving your child five positive comments for every negative comment.

7. If you think you might need a refresher course on parenting skills, you're not alone. Many parents today seek advice and insights from other parents and trained professionals. Check your local bookshop, children's centre or library for parenting books or courses. See whether your child's school holds parenting discussions, programmes, or workshops; find out what's available in your community. The more you learn, the more you know!

8. If you think you might need more help than you can get from a book, programme or workshop on parenting, and especially if you feel that your child is developing problem behaviours, get professional help. Ask the school, your local children's centre, a behavioural psychologist, your GP or social worker for recommendations. There's no shame in this; it takes wisdom and courage to acknowledge that you can't do it all.

If you feel that you sometimes over-react and would like to learn ways to control your emotions, visit your local library or bookshop and look for books on managing stress and handling challenging kids. Ask other teachers what they do when they feel like they're about to blow up. Meanwhile:

- Remember that you're the adult, then behave like one.

- Tell yourself that you'll stay calm no matter what.

- Learn and practise simple relaxation techniques you can use when pupils push you to the edge of your patience.

- Make an agreement with another teacher whose classroom is near yours. Whenever one of you reaches the end of your rope, you can ask the other to take over your class for a few minutes while you go to a quiet place and regain control of your emotions. Or you can send a pupil who's driving you crazy to the other teacher's room for a short period of time.

What if a bully threatens you? Try not to look angry, upset or afraid. Don't grab the pupil. Don't raise your voice. Don't set up a power struggle by challenging him or her. Don't cross your arms and shout across the room. Don't verbally attack the pupil and back him or her into a corner by demanding immediate compliance.

Instead, remain calm, confident, assertive and under control. Keep your body language and facial expression neutral. Speak clearly in your normal tone of voice as you move closer to the pupil (no closer than arm's length), state your expectations and give the pupil a choice: stop the behaviour and accept the consequences, or continue the behaviour and bring on worse consequences. If the pupil wants to argue, simply restate the choice.

Tip: If you feel that you might be in real danger, get reinforcements – another teacher or the head-teacher.* In extreme cases of bullying where anyone is at risk from harm, it may well be relevant to contact the police.

HAVE CLEAR CONSEQUENCES IN PLACE

If your school or local authority already has consequences in place for bullying behaviours, familiarise yourself with them. Communicate them to pupils and parents so everyone knows what they are.

- You might summarise the consequences simply and clearly on a poster for your classroom.

- Create a handout for pupils; send copies home or give them to parents during conferences, open houses, or Parents' Evening.

- If your school publishes a pupil or parent handbook or brochure, the consequences should be included there.

Consequences are essential because they tell you exactly how to follow through when a pupil behaves inappropriately. You know which behaviours are grounds for a warning, reprimand, time-out, in-school detention, dismissal, suspension and (a last resort) expulsion. You don't have to decide what to do each time a bullying situation arises; uncertainty is replaced by consistency, and there are no surprises for anyone.

What if your school or local authority hasn't spelled out specific consequences for bullying behaviours? Form a team of other teachers and teaching assistants and work together to determine consequences that are:

- *practical* (doable where you are and with the resources available to you)

- *logical* (they make sense and are related to specific bullying behaviours)

- *reasonable and fair* (excessively punitive consequences 'bully the bully')

- *inevitable* (if a pupil does A, then B happens – no exceptions)

---

* See also 'Protect Yourself'' (page 110–111).

- *predictable* (everyone in the school community knows that A leads to B)

- *immediate* (consequences are applied at the earliest possible opportunity)

- *escalating* (continuing the behaviour leads to more serious consequences)

- *consistently enforced* (if two students do A, then B happens for both)

- *developmentally appropriate and age-appropriate* (the consequences for name-calling in Year 3 will be different from the consequences for name-calling in Year 6).

Tip: Consider including pupils on your team or involve the school council. Since bullying affects them directly, they'll have a personal interest and commitment to the process, and they'll bring their unique perspective to the table.

At your team's first meeting, you might want to share the following advice.* Use it as a starting point for determining consequences for bullying behaviours:

> *Discipline practices should emphasise restitution and positive practice rather than expulsion and humiliation. That is, when pupils are caught bullying they should apologise, demonstrate the correct behaviour and then have to spend a specified period of time helping younger, less able children ... Although it is very difficult to justify, bullies should not be removed from the school setting unless absolutely necessary.*

ONE SCHOOL'S STORY
The staff at one school perceived that informal pupil interactions in the playground and on the bus included too much teasing and too many put-downs. After lengthy discussions about the negative effects of hurtful comments, they developed a zero tolerance standard to eliminate name-calling and insults.

Pupils who called others names were sent to the school office to call home and tell their parents what they had done. Consequences were spelled out for infractions that continued or escalated. Teachers volunteered extra-duty periods to implement the new standard and establish the expectation: no name-calling.

Some people thought the standard seemed extreme. During the first month or so, the office saw a virtual parade of pupils for lunchtime detention. But it didn't take long for pupils to adjust, and today the change in school climate is noteworthy; only a few pupils each week get into trouble. When pupils were surveyed about the programme, one wrote, "I don't have to worry about zero tolerance because I don't use those words."*

APOLOGIES AND AMENDS
Although opinions differ on whether bullies should apologise to their targets, saying "I'm sorry" is the first step towards recognising that a behaviour is inappropriate and taking responsibility for that behaviour. Many bullies blame the target ("he/she made me do it", "he/she deserved it") and see no need to apologise. Don't listen to excuses; simply insist that the bully apologise – verbally or in writing. If he or she refuses, apply appropriate consequences for his or her lack of cooperation.

Beyond apologising to the target, the pupil should also make amends for his or her behaviour. *Examples*:

- For every 'put-down' comment the pupil makes about another, he or she should make one or more 'build-up' comment.

- If the pupil extorted money, he or she should pay it back as soon as possible. Also consider having the pupil do work around the

---

* SOURCE: 'Bullying Fact Sheet' by George Batsche and Benjamin Moore, in *Helping Children Grow Up in the '90s: A Resource Book for Parents and Teachers* (Bethesda, MD: National Association of School Psychologists, 1992).

---

* SOURCE: 'Respect among peers is a goal of Wayne policy' by Janet Adelberg, *The Chalkboard*, December 1998.

school (in the media centre, office etc.) for half an hour every day for one week.

- If the pupil damaged or destroyed something belonging to another, he or she should repair or replace it as soon as possible.

TIME-OUTS

The time-out is a time-honoured way to modify pupils' behaviour – or at least put a stop to inappropriate behaviour and give tempers a chance to cool.

Tell pupils when time-outs will be used, and describe the specific behaviours that will lead to a time-out. Establish a time-out place in your classroom – a special area away from the group where pupils can be seen and supervised. In contrast to the rest of your classroom, try to keep the time-out place relatively dull and boring – no fun posters, no books or toys.

As you use time-outs with your pupils, keep these general guidelines in mind:

- A time-out is not a detention. Rather, it's time spent away from the group and its activities, social feedback and rewards.

- A time-out is not a punishment. It's an opportunity for a pupil to calm down and ponder his or her behaviour.

- A time-out is brief. A few minutes is usually sufficient – longer for more serious or disruptive behaviours, but no more than 10–15 minutes.

- A time-out is not to be used for classwork or homework. (Nor should it be used by the pupil as an opportunity to get out of an assignment or classwork he or she doesn't want to do.)

- A time-out is not a battleground. Don't argue with the pupil. Don't engage in any kind of conversation with the pupil. Simply say, "You (broke a particular class rule or violated a guideline), and that's a time-out. Please go to the time-out place right now."

- What if a pupil refuses to go to the time-out place? Try adding one or two minutes to the time-out for each minute the pupil delays going. Or you might say, "For every minute you put off going to time-out, that's five minutes you'll have to stay in from breaktime."

- When a time-out is over, it's over. The pupil returns to the group without criticism, comments or conditions.

Tip: Consider giving pupils the option to put *themselves* on a time-out when they feel they are about to behave inappropriately. This empowers pupils to make good choices on their own behalf and teaches them to remove themselves from a potentially volatile situation.

CHANGE THEIR THINKING

As you work to help bullies, it's as important to change their *thinking* as it is to change their behaviour. Bullies often deny that they've done anything wrong and refuse to take responsibility for their behaviour. They believe that their actions are someone else's 'fault'. Or they dismiss them as "no big deal" or insist that they were "misinterpreted".* You'll need to challenge their thinking without preaching.

1. Ask them to consider this question and respond verbally or in writing:

   If you think you're *not* bullying another person, but that person thinks you *are*, who's right?

   Lead pupils to understand that bullying is in the 'eye of the beholder' – that the other person's feelings and fears are real to him or her.

2. Suggest that there are three ways to look at any situation involving two people:

   - my interpretation – what I think happened and why

---

* See 'Warning Signs' (pages 118–119).

- your interpretation – what you think happened and why

- the facts – what really happened.

Sometimes it helps if there's a third person present (a bystander or witness) who's objective and can give his or her view of the facts.

3. Have pupils keep a diary of events that upset, frustrate or anger them.* For each event, they should write a brief, factual description, followed by their own interpretation of what happened.

Review and discuss their diary entries one-on-one or in small group discussions. Encourage pupils to look for possible errors in their interpretations. *Example*: Maybe what happened was an accident. Maybe they misinterpreted something that wasn't meant to upset them. Maybe *they* caused the problem.

 Go further:
For a list of thinking errors and the correct social thinking, see *Bully-Proofing Your School: A Comprehensive Approach for Elementary Schools* by Carla Garrity, Kathryn Jens, William Porter, Nancy Sager and Cam Short-Camilli (Longmont, CO: Sopris West, 1996).

4. Help pupils self-identify. The 'Are You Bullying Others?' handout (page 128) will start them thinking about their own behaviour. You might give these only to pupils you know or suspect are bullying others. Or make this a whole-class exercise, followed by discussion. Even pupils who don't bully can benefit from examining some of their own attitudes and behaviours.

 Important:
Collect the completed handouts and keep them confidential.

* See also 'Weekly Diary' (pages 42–43).

COMMUNICATE WITH PARENTS

Once you've informed a pupil's parents that their child is or may be bullying others, it's essential to follow through with regular communication and updates on their child's progress. It's normal for parents to be defensive at first, perhaps even angry that their child has been identified as a 'problem' pupil. You can help to allay their fears, calm their worries, lower their defences, build trust and increase their willingness to cooperate by promising to stay in touch and keeping your promise.

You probably already communicate with your pupils' parents – in parent consultations, at open days and parents' evenings, with notes home and in other ways. Here are a few more ideas to consider:

- Pick up the phone and call parents, or let them know the best times to call you. Offer alternatives – before school, after school, during lunch or break times.

- Each day, write comments on a note card about the child's behaviour in school and send it home with the child. (For privacy, put the card in a sealed envelope.) Make sure to write at least as many positive comments as negative comments (if possible, write *more* positives than negatives). You might put a star by each positive comment. Suggest to parents that when a child has earned a certain number of stars for the week, they might offer the child a reward – doing something special with Mum or Dad, choosing a film to watch, having a friend spend the night. *Tip*: For the first few days, you might follow through with a phone call to make sure your notes are getting into parents' hands and not being 'lost' on the way home from school.

- If both you and the parents have access to email, this is a fast and easy way to stay in touch.

Depending on the situation, you can also have the pupil communicate directly with his or her own parents. *Example*: If Kevin calls Marcus a name, have Kevin write a note describing what he said and what happened afterwards. Kevin might write, "I called Marcus a bad name in school. First Ms Sellick said to apologise to Marcus. I said I was sorry. Then she put me on a time-out. I thought about how Marcus felt when I called him the bad name. I won't do it again." Read the note before it goes home; check to make sure that the pupil has taken responsibility for his or her behaviour (as opposed to "Marcus is a !@#$%" or "I got in trouble because Stefan told on me"). Follow through with a phone call to make sure parents receive the note.

As the pupil progresses, daily communication can eventually become weekly communication, then twice monthly, and so on until the problem behaviours have greatly improved or stopped altogether.

GET PARENTS TOGETHER

When you first inform parents that their children are bullying others or being bullied, you'll want to meet *separately* with each set of parents (or carers). It's hard enough for parents to hear this kind of news without having to face the parents of the child who is hurting their son or daughter (or being hurt by him or her). It's tempting to go on the offensive or become defensive, and suddenly you have another set of problems on your hands.

In time, however, and especially if you're making progress helping both pupils, you might want to consider getting the parents together for a face-to-face meeting. You might want to include the educational psychologist.

 Important:
Use your judgment, follow your instincts and ask the parents (separately) how they feel about this. Are they ready to sit down and talk to each other? Can they set aside

their negative feelings – anger, disappointment, fear, hostility – and keep an open mind? Can they agree to hear both sides? Can they present a united front of caring adults who all want the best for their children?

When parents are willing to communicate and work together, this brings a special energy to the situation. Pupils who are having difficulty getting along see a good example: adults on opposite sides of a problem who are willing to talk and work together. This gives both sets of parents the opportunity to serve as positive role models.

KEEP THE FOCUS ON BEHAVIOUR

In your interactions with a pupil who bullies others, be sure to emphasise that the problem is the *behaviour*, not the pupil himself or herself.

Never label the pupil a 'bully'. Instead of saying, "I've noticed that you're a bully" or "People tell me you're a bully" or "You must stop being a bully," say something like "Hitting (or kicking, teasing, excluding, name-calling etc.) is a bullying behaviour, and it is not allowed in our classroom." Or "There are lots of good things I like about you – your smile, your talent for drawing, and your sense of humour. But I don't like it when you tease other pupils, and we need to work on that behaviour." For every negative statement you make to point out an undesirable behaviour, try to include one or more positives.

When you need to remove a pupil from a situation, be specific about your reasons for doing so. *Example*: "Jon, I'm putting you on time-out because you shoved Tracy, and shoving isn't allowed." Make sure the pupil knows why he or she is being removed. Ask, "Why am I putting you on time-out?" If the pupil offers excuses ("Tracy shoved me first" or "I didn't mean to shove her" or "It was an accident"), calmly restate your reason ("I'm putting you on time-out because you shoved Tracy, and shoving isn't allowed"). Ask the pupil to reflect on his or her reasons for being removed.

ARE YOU BULLYING OTHERS?

Have you ever wondered whether you might be bullying others? Here's a quick way to tell whether you are or might be. Read each question and circle 'Y' (for yes) or 'N' (for no). When you're finished, give this handout to the teacher.

Be honest! Your answers will be kept private.

1. Do you pick on people who are smaller than you, or on animals?   Y   N

2. Do you like to tease and taunt other people?   Y   N

3. If you tease people, do you like to see them get upset?   Y   N

4. Do you think it's funny when other people make mistakes?   Y   N

5. Do you like to take or destroy other people's belongings?   Y   N

6. Do you want other pupils to think you're the toughest child in school?   Y   N

7. Do you get angry a lot and stay angry for a long time?   Y   N

8. Do you blame other people for things that go wrong in your life?   Y   N

9. Do you like to get revenge on people who hurt you?   Y   N

10. When you play a game or sport, do you always have to be the winner?   Y   N

11. If you lose at something, do you worry about what other people will think of you?   Y   N

12. Do you get angry or jealous when someone else succeeds?   Y   N

Read this AFTER you answer all of the questions!

If you answered 'Yes' to one or two of these questions, you may be on your way to bullying others. If you answered 'Yes' to three or more, you probably are bullying others, and you need to find ways to change your behaviour. Good news: you can get help dealing with your feelings, getting along with other people and making friends. Parents, teachers and other adults can all give this kind of help. JUST ASK!!!

You might even use an old-fashioned technique and have the pupil write the reason on paper – 25 times? 50 times? ("I'm on time-out because I shoved Tracy, and shoving isn't allowed.")

Take every opportunity to show your approval and acceptance of the pupil as a *person*. Separate the pupil from the behaviour. *Example*: "Shawna, you know I like you a lot. But I don't like it when you pick on kids who are smaller than you. Let's talk about ways you can change that behaviour."

TEACH PUPILS TO MONITOR THEIR OWN BEHAVIOUR

Have pupils who bully others monitor their own behaviour. Work with each pupil to identify and list inappropriate behaviours he or she needs to change. The pupil then keeps a tally of how often he or she engages in each behaviour. Or, to cast this in a more positive light, the pupil can record the amount of time (in 15-minute intervals or number of class periods) during which he or she *doesn't* engage in the behaviour. Either way, this deliberate, conscientious record-keeping usually leads to greater control over one's behaviour. *Tip*: The pupil must *want* to change the behaviours, or self-monitoring won't work.

PROVIDE COUNSELLING

Pupils who bully others need help learning how to relate to their peers in more positive, productive ways. If at all possible, they should have access to some type of counselling – by a trained adult. In some cases, peer counselling can also be useful. Some experts feel that counselling or discussion with pupils involved in bullying should occur *before* consequences are applied.

Counselling groups have a big advantage over punishment or other disciplinary tactics, although they shouldn't take the place of reasonable and consistent consequences for specific behaviours. Rather than driving the problem underground, groups bring it out in the open where pupils can discuss it and adults can offer their input and advice. Rather than making bullies feel even more excluded and socially inept, groups offer opportunities for pupils to talk about what's bothering them, explore reasons for their behaviour and learn alternatives to bullying others.

In general, bullies don't 'outgrow' their problem without some type of professional help. Often, it's not enough to counsel only the bully – especially if his or her inappropriate behaviours were learned at home. During your discussions with the pupil's parents, you might suggest they consider family counselling. Have a list of local and community resources available for parents who seem willing to give it a try.

GET OTHER PUPILS INVOLVED

Never underestimate the power of peer pressure! As you're helping bullies change their behaviour, get the whole class involved.*

In some schools, pupils have formed 'good gangs' to defend targets of bullies. When they see someone being mistreated (perhaps when the teacher's back is turned), they shout in unison at the pupil who's doing the bullying: "Leave (target's name) alone!" You might role-play this with your class to see how it works.

Have pupils practise things they might say to friends who bully others. *Examples*: "If you want me to keep being your friend, you have to stop teasing Paul." "I don't like it when my friends hurt other people." "When you hit Raisa, that makes *me* feel bad and I don't want to be around you."

When you notice bullying behaviour, call pupils' attention to it. You might say, "Look at what Ben just did to Alex. He threw his notebook on the floor. That's not fair, is it? What can we do to help?" Then encourage pupils to act on a valid suggestion (helping Alex pick up his notebook; telling Ben to cut it out).

Give pupils permission to point out when someone is breaking a class rule (see 'Set Rules', pages

---

* See also 'Mobilise Bystanders' (pages 93 and 97).

33–34). *Example*: A pupil might say, "Class Rule Number Two! We don't tease people."

Go further:
Ask pupils to brainstorm ways to express their intolerance for bullying behaviour. Write their ideas on the board and invite class discussion. They might vote for their top five ideas, then create a poster titled 'Ways to Combat Bullying'.

HELP PUPILS IDENTIFY AND PURSUE THEIR INTERESTS

It's often true that pupils who bully others don't have special interests or hobbies. They spend much of their time picking on others, planning ways to pick on others or responding to imagined slights or offences. Because they tend to be very competitive and are poor losers, they may choose not to get involved in activities where there's a chance they won't excel or win.

Identify pupils who are bullies or potential bullies (see pages 117 and 120), then make time to talk to them one-on-one. Explain that you'd like to get to know them better. Ask them what they like to do in their free time; don't be surprised if they can't (or won't) answer right away. They may be suspicious or defensive. Be patient, friendly, welcoming and warm; back off if you sense that a pupil feels uncomfortable.

You might guide them with questions like the following.* *Tip*: Along the way, share information about your own interests and hobbies, as appropriate. The discussion shouldn't be about *you*, but if you're willing to reveal a little about your life, pupils might follow your example and let you in on theirs.

1. Do you like to read books or magazines? What are your favourites? Do you have a favourite time to read? A special place where you like to curl up or sprawl out and read?

2. What do you like to watch on TV?

3. Have you seen any good films lately? What are your favourite films or DVDs? What do you like about them?

4. What's your favourite kind of music? Who are your favourite groups or bands?

5. What's your favourite way to let off steam? Do you run? Bike? Skate? Play football?

6. When you have free time at home, what do you like to do best? Do you have a hobby? Tell me about it.

7. How much time do you spend on your hobby? What do you like most about it?

8. Imagine that you have all the money and all the freedom in the world. What's *one* thing you'd really like to do?

9. What do you think you might want to be when you grow up?

10. Imagine that you could go anywhere in the world. Where would you like to go? Why? What would you do there?

11. Imagine that you could be anyone in the world – past, present or future. Who would you be? Why would you want to be that person? What would you do if you were that person?

12. Is there something you've always wanted to try? What about (acting in a play, starting a collection, singing in a band, playing on a team, joining a club, playing a musical instrument, dancing, working with animals etc.)?

If you learn that the pupil has a hobby, encourage him or her to tell you more about it. If it's a collection, maybe the pupil can bring all or part of it to school and share it with the class.

If you learn that the pupil has a special interest (or the potential to develop a special interest), offer to help him or her pursue it. Put the pupil in touch with people or organisations in your school and community.* Offer encouragement and follow

---

* See also 'Learn More About Your Pupils' (pages 42–43).

* See also 'Encourage Relationships with Other Adults' (page 106).

through by asking questions about his or her progress and experiences as the year goes on.

TEACH LEADERSHIP SKILLS

Bullies are skilled at getting and using power over others. They do it for the wrong reasons (to intimidate and control), in the wrong ways (with physical force, verbal abuse or emotional manipulation) and to the wrong ends (victimising others and making them miserable), but clearly they possess real ability. Why not channel all that talent into something worthwhile?

Consider offering leadership training especially for pupils who have been identified as bullies or potential bullies. Check to see what's available in your locality through organisations that serve children and youth.*

Good leadership training promotes and strengthens many positive character traits and skills. *Examples*:

- activism
- admitting mistakes
- assertiveness
- being a good sport
- caring
- citizenship
- coaching
- communication
- compromise
- concern
- confidence
- conflict resolution
- cooperation
- courage
- creativity
- credibility
- decision-making
- dedication
- delegating
- dependability
- endurance
- enthusiasm
- fairness
- follow-through
- goal-setting
- honesty
- imagination
- independence
- influencing others
- ingenuity
- initiative
- inspiring others
- integrity
- judgment
- justice
- learning
- listening
- loyalty
- motivating others
- patience
- perseverance
- planning
- positive attitudes
- positive risk-taking
- pride
- purpose
- resiliency
- resourcefulness
- respect for others
- responsibility
- self-awareness
- self-esteem
- self-improvement
- self-respect
- service to others
- setting a good example
- tact
- team-building
- thoughtfulness
- trustworthiness
- unselfishness

Imagine what might happen if we could turn bullies into leaders! It's worth a try . . . and it could turn troublemaking pupils into contributing assets to our schools and communities.

HELP PUPILS FIND MENTORS

Pupils who bully others are pupils at risk for serious problems now and in the future. It's a proven fact that pupils at risk can be helped to improve their behaviour and stay out of trouble by being matched with mentors – adults or teens who care about them and spend time with them.

In 1992 and 1993, Public/Private Ventures (P/PV), a US research organisation based in Philadelphia, studied the effects of mentoring during an 18-month experiment involving nearly 1000 boys and girls aged 10–16 in eight states.* Half of the children were matched with mentors through Big Brothers Big Sisters of America (BBBSA) agencies; half were assigned to a waiting list or control group. The children in the first group met with their Big Brothers/Sisters about three times a month for at least a year.

At the end of the study, P/PV found that the mentored pupils were:

_____

* See 'Clubs, Groups and Teams' (page 106).

_____

* SOURCE: 'Mentoring – A Proven Delinquency Prevention Strategy' by Jean Baldwin Grossman and Eileen M. Garry (Washington, DC: US Department of Justice, Office of Juvenile Justice and Delinquency Prevention), April 1997.

- **46% less likely** than the pupils in the control groups to start using illegal drugs

- **27% less likely** to start using alcohol

- **53% less likely** to skip school

- **37% less likely** to skip a class

- **almost 33% less likely to hit someone**

- **getting along better with their peers**

- **getting along better with their parents.**

You can make a big difference in the life of any pupil by matching him or her with a mentor. For more information about mentoring see the Peer Support page on the Kidscape website: www.kidscape.org.uk/training/peersupport.shtml.

You can also ask other teachers in your school if they would be willing to mentor pupils in your classroom who need more positive interaction with adults. (At the same time, you might offer to mentor a pupil in another teacher's classroom.)

For more about mentoring, see page 106.

LEARN MORE ABOUT YOUR PUPILS

Learn as much as you can about the bullies or potential bullies in your classroom.* Show interest in them as individuals – as people worth knowing. Make it clear that even though you don't like some of their behaviours,** you still value them as human beings. You want them to succeed, and you care about their future.

LEARN ABOUT THEM

- Meet them individually or in small groups as often as you can. You might start by meeting weekly, then twice a month, then monthly.

- Show interest in their lives and be a good listener (see pages 90–92).

- Communicate your high expectations for them – and your confidence that they can meet your expectations.

- Point out and praise the positive behaviours you've noticed, and encourage them to keep up the good work. Let them know that you're keeping an eye on them – and you want to 'catch them being good'.*

- You might also mention the negative behaviours you've noticed and remind them of why these behaviours are not acceptable, but don't dwell on these. This isn't the time. 'Learn More' meetings should focus on positive qualities, characteristics and behaviours as much as possible.

LEARN ABOUT THEIR FAMILIES

- Ask pupils about their families. You might have them write essays, poems, stories, songs or short plays about their families. If your pupils are keeping diaries (see pages 42–43), you might ask them to write about their families in their diaries.

- Hold regular consultations with their parents; you might include the pupils, too. Observe the interactions between parents and children. If you sense that the parents don't like you or trust you – perhaps because they see you as part of the problem – try to find out whether there's another teacher or teaching assistant they do like and trust. Ask whether they're willing to meet that person instead.

- Ask the parents whether it's okay to visit them at home. This will give you a better understanding of how the pupils' family

---

* See also 'Learn More About Your Pupils' (pages 42–43) and 'Help Pupils Identify and Pursue Their Interests' (pages 130–131).

** See also 'Keep the Focus on Behaviour' (pages 127 and 129).

* See also 'Catch Them in the Act' (pages 114–115).

experiences might be affecting their behaviour at school.

CAMPAIGN AGAINST BULLYING

One way to help bullies change their behaviour is to make it clear that bullying won't be tolerated in your classroom. When you and the majority of your pupils present a united front against bullying, bullies find it harder to behave in ways that are obviously unwanted, undesirable and unpopular.

The 'Creating a Positive Classroom' section of this book includes many tips and strategies that can discourage bullies from bullying – and encourage them to explore more positive ways of relating to others. You might also conduct an all-out campaign against bullying. Have your pupils work together (as a class or in small groups) to create posters, banners, jingles, short plays, raps, songs etc. around one or more anti-bullying themes. *Examples*:

- Bullying isn't cool.
- Kindness is cool.
- Acceptance is cool.
- Tolerance is cool.
- We stand up for ourselves and each other.
- In our classroom, no one is an outsider.
- In our classroom, everyone is welcome.
- We treat others the way we want to be treated.
- Spreading rumours isn't cool.
- Gossip isn't cool.
- Name-calling isn't cool.
- New pupils are welcome here.

- No one ever deserves to be bullied.
- Everyone is unique.
- Hurray for differences!
- No teasing allowed.
- If we see someone being bullied, we're telling!
- Telling isn't wrong.
- Reporting is helping.
- Bullying? No way! There's always a better way.

Or have pupils brainstorm anti-bullying themes, then choose one they'd like to work on.

Go further:
Ask groups of pupils to research successful advertising campaigns, then try to determine what made them successful. Did the campaigns have catchy slogans? Appealing graphics? Popular spokespersons? Songs or jingles that were easy to remember? Ask pupils to create anti-bullying campaigns based on what they learned from their research. You might even have a schoolwide competition, with the winning campaign adopted by the whole school. Keep your local media (newspapers, magazines, radio stations, TV stations) informed about the competition and the winner.

HELP PUPILS MANAGE THEIR ANGER

Pupils who bully others have a hard time managing their anger. That's one reason they bully. They need help learning how to control their temper, curb violent or aggressive impulses, and resist taking out their anger on others.

Have one-on-one conversations with pupils who bully others – or who might not be bullies but seem to have difficulty managing their anger. Or you might have a class discussion on this topic.

Ask questions like the following. If you prefer, you might adapt these questions for a worksheet. Have pupils complete it in class or as a homework assignment. Then review their responses and meet individually or in small groups with pupils who seem to need help.

1. How can you tell when you're angry? What do you do?

2. How do you feel when you're angry? Hurt? Misunderstood? Frustrated? Sad? Hot all over? Like you're about to explode? Like you want to strike out at someone else?

3. Describe a time when you were very angry. How did you feel? What did you do? What happened next? How did you feel afterwards?

4. How do you feel when someone gets angry at you? Are you scared? Upset? Do you wish you could just disappear?

5. Do you think it's fair when someone else takes out his or her anger on you?

6. How does your anger affect the people around you? What about your family? Friends? The person or people you're angry at? How do you think they feel when you take out your anger on them?

7. Is there anything you'd like to change about the way you feel and act when you get angry?

8. Would you like to learn different ways to act when you get angry?

With your pupils, brainstorm ideas for managing anger. Write their ideas on the board. Afterwards, have pupils choose one idea to work on for the next few days, then report back to you on whether it works for them. Here are some starter ideas:*

• Learn to recognise the signs that you're about to explode. Do something *before* you explode.

• Walk away from the person or situation that's making you angry. You're not running away. You're doing something positive to make sure things don't get worse or out of control.

• Take five deep breaths. Take five more.

• Count to ten s-l-o-w-l-y. Do it again if you need to.

• Let off steam in a safe, positive way. Go for a run. Take a bike ride. Jump up and down.

• Make yourself relax and cool down. Think calm, peaceful thoughts. Try tensing, then relaxing every muscle in your body, from your head to your toes.

• Pretend that you're not angry. You may do such a good acting job that you convince yourself.

• Ask yourself, "Why am I angry?" Maybe the person didn't mean to make you angry. Maybe it was an accident or a misunderstanding.

• Try not to take things so personally. Understand that the whole world isn't against you.

 Go further:
Talk with your SENCO or educational psychologist about starting an anger management group for pupils. The group might meet during breaktime or lunch – times that are otherwise unstructured.

GET OLDER PUPILS INVOLVED

Often, pupils who bully others find it easier to talk and work with older pupils than with adults. If possible, arrange for the older pupils in your school to mentor younger ones.

---

* See also 'Teach Anger Management Skills' (page 35).

USE 'STOP AND THINK'

Most teachers have developed a 'sixth sense' when it comes to pupil behaviour. They can detect a problem before it occurs and act quickly to prevent it. Sometimes all it takes is a look or a word from the teacher to get pupils back on track.

'Stop and Think' takes this a step further. Not only does it interrupt inappropriate behaviour, it also invites pupils to consider what they're doing (or about to do) and make a better choice.

Here are three ways to use 'Stop and Think' in your classroom:

1. Tell your pupils, "You have the power to *stop and think* before you speak or act. This is a way to keep yourself from saying or doing something that might get you into trouble or hurt someone else. Whenever I say 'Stop and Think', I want the person or people I'm addressing to do just that. STOP whatever you're saying or doing. Then THINK about what you're about to say or do. Decide whether you should say or do something else instead."

Once you've introduced 'Stop and Think', use this short, simple phrase whenever necessary. Keep your voice calm and your expression positive or neutral. (This is a great alternative to yelling or other emotional responses.)

2. Distribute copies of the handout on page 138. Have pupils colour in the stop sign and thought bubble, then cut along the dark solid line, fold along the dotted line and tape or staple the top together.

   Younger pupils might want to wear their 'Stop/Think' signs as necklaces (punch two holes in the top corners, then weave a length of yarn or string through the holes). Older pupils can carry their signs in their pockets.

   Tell your pupils, "You have the power to *stop and think* before you speak or act. Your 'Stop/Think' sign can remind you to do this."

3. Give pupils permission to use 'Stop and Think' with each other. Enlist their help in interrupting impulsive or negative behaviours.

GIVE PUPILS MEANINGFUL RESPONSIBILITIES

As you're planning special class projects and events, try giving some of the most meaningful and desirable tasks to pupils who might otherwise use their time and energy bullying others.* Make sure these are tasks that really matter, and let pupils know you're counting on them to do their best.

Tip: If you know that a younger pupil is being bullied on the playground, consider assigning one of your class 'bullies' as that child's protector. Talk this over with your pupil ahead of time; emphasise that he or she is not to bully the child's bully. Your pupil's presence might be enough to dissuade the child's bully from picking on him or her.

TEACH THEM TO 'TALK SENSE TO THEMSELVES'

Schools can have rules and anti-bullying policies, adults can determine and apply consequences, but ultimately each pupil must learn to control his or her own inappropriate and/or impulsive behaviours.

Just as pupils can learn positive self-talk (see pages 76–77), they can also learn to 'talk sense to themselves' – to talk themselves *out of* behaviours that are likely to hurt someone else and/or get them into trouble, and *into* behaviours that are more desirable and acceptable.

Work with your pupils one-on-one or in small groups to come up with brief, powerful, easy-to-remember words and phrases they can use to 'talk sense to themselves'. *Examples*:

---

* See also 'Give Them Opportunities to Shine' (page 108).

- **I don't have to do this.**
- **I can make a better choice.**
- **I can keep my hands to myself.**
- **I can walk away.**
- **I can control myself.**
- **There's a better way.**
- **I'm better than this.**
- **I'm in charge of me.**
- **I can stop and think.**
- **I can put on the brakes.**

Have pupils choose their favourite word or phrase, then write it on an index card and carry it in their pocket. Tell them to think (or whisper) their phrase whenever they feel they might say or do something to hurt another person.

COMPILE BEHAVIOUR PROFILES

For each pupil who exhibits bullying behaviours, create a Behaviour Profile in a special folder.

Throughout the day and/or at the end of the day, jot down detailed notes about the pupil's behaviour.

 Important:
Be sure to include positive as well as negative behaviours.

Use the folder to collect and store notes and reports you receive from other pupils, teachers and staff about the pupil's behaviour; notes taken during meetings and conversations with the pupil's parents; and anything else you feel is meaningful and relevant.

Towards the end of each week, review and summarise the Behaviour Profile. Has the pupil's behaviour improved during the week? Are there areas that still need work? What strategies and techniques did you try to help the pupil? Which ones were most effective? If the pupil behaved inappropriately, what consequences were applied? Did the consequences have the desired effect?

Share pertinent information from your Behaviour Profile with the pupil, his or her parents (through a phone call or a note home) and other staff members involved in helping the pupil improve his or her behaviour.

Tip: Careful notes can be very useful during parent-teacher consultations and any other meetings where the child is the focus.

TEACH POSITIVE WAYS TO FEEL POWERFUL

Offer bullies positive ways to channel their need for power. Here are ten examples and ideas to try:

1. In one school, teachers learned that an older pupil was harassing younger pupils. The teacher took the bully aside, told him that someone was picking on the little children in the school, and asked him to help. The bully became a guardian.

2. In another school, bullies were sent to clean up the reception classroom as a subtle form of punishment. The reception pupils then wrote thank-you notes to the bullies – a not-so-subtle form of praise that made the bullies feel good about themselves.

3. Consider having bullies hand out awards to pupils who have done good deeds, helped other pupils or otherwise set positive examples for others to emulate.

4. There's power in correcting mistakes and righting wrongs. Emphasise that mistakes are for learning and wrongs are opportunities to step forward, be a leader and win well-deserved admiration from peers and adults.

5. Assign bullies to watch out for and help pupils who are especially timid or shy. Encourage them to feel good about protecting their new friends.

6. Some experts suggest holding bullies responsible for the safety and well-being of their targets. If something happens to their targets, the bullies suffer the consequences – even if someone else did the deed.

7. Encourage (even require) bullies to get involved in school activities – plays, sports, clubs etc. Do everything in your power to ensure that their experiences are positive and successful. If they aren't interested in any of the activities currently available, offer to help them start a club or group of their choosing. Participating gives pupils a sense of belonging, which helps them feel valued – and powerful.

8. Ask your school counsellor or educational psychologist to assess bullies' self-esteem. It's a myth that all bullies have low self-esteem (in fact, some have *high* self-esteem), but it's worth checking into. If bullies are found to have low self-esteem, start a group or programme to help them.

9. Doing good by helping others is a powerful feeling.

10. Invite bullies to brainstorm their own ideas for being powerful without hurting or intimidating others. Express confidence in their ability to come up with good strategies.

TRY CRITICAL QUESTIONING

Immediately after intervening with a bullying incident (removing the audience, removing the bully and giving the bully a few moments to calm down), ask the bully a series of questions that require him or her to reflect on the incident. *Examples*:

1. What just happened? (Insist on 'just the facts' – no excuses, no rationalisations, no blaming the target.)

2. What exactly did you do? (Not *why*, just *what*.)

3. What will happen next for you? (Remind the pupil of the consequences of his or her behaviour.)

4. How do you feel right now?

5. How do you think the other person feels?

6. Is this really what you wanted to happen?

7. What could you do next time instead of (hitting, kicking, name-calling, teasing or whatever occurred)?

8. How can you make sure something like this doesn't happen again? What can you do?

PROVIDE A PLACE FOR PUPILS TO GO

If at all possible, set aside a room in your school where pupils who bully others can be sent to calm down and consider their behaviour.

You might call this the Resource Room, the library or anything else that sets it apart from a regular classroom (and doesn't obviously label it 'the place where bullies go'). Staff it with a teacher or teaching assistant who can work with pupils, talk to them, provide structured activities, listen to their concerns, and help them learn and practise positive ways of relating to others.

Going to this special room might be a consequence of bullying behaviour, or a choice pupils can make for themselves when they feel they're losing control.

INTERVIEW THOSE INVOLVED

Both bullies and targets of bullying can be interviewed about what has been reported – preferably as soon as possible after the incident. You need bullies to acknowledge their actions and, better still, suggest a solution to the situation. If this

1. Cut along the outer line

2. Fold on the dotted line

does not happen, further (usually punitive) actions will need to be taken to make it clear to bullies that what they did was unacceptable. Guidelines for interviewing bullies can be found on page 104.

Interviewing targets can be useful to ascertain whether or not they think there might be a solution to the bullying. It also consolidates the idea that the school takes bullying very seriously. Sample interviews with two different types of target can be found on page 105.

HELP PUPILS UNDERSTAND WHY THEY BULLY OTHERS

If you can help bullies to *recognise* that they behave inappropriately and take *responsibility* for their behaviour,* you can start to help them *realise* why they do the things they do.

This activity and the 'Reasons Why' questionnaire (pages 141–142) may not be appropriate for some pupils. Some questions may be too complex or confusing for their age or developmental level. Use your judgment and your knowledge of your pupils; adapt where appropriate – or come up with other questions you think will work better. If you use this questionnaire, be sure to tell your pupils that this isn't a test. There are no 'right' or 'wrong' answers – only answers that are true for them and may not be true for anyone else.

Important:
Consider inviting the SENCO to join you for this activity. He or she will be a valuable resource. Also: this activity should precede 'Help Pupils Stop Bullying' (following). If you decide to use the 'Reasons Why' questionnaire, be sure to follow through with 'Reasons Why (Guidance Questions)' (pages 143–144).

Depending on your pupils' ages and abilities, they can complete the 'Reasons Why' handout and turn it in to you, or you might choose to go over the questions one at a time during a face-to-face meeting or small group discussion.

HELP PUPILS STOP BULLYING

This activity should follow 'Help Pupils Understand Why They Bully Others' (preceding). If you haven't yet done that activity, please read through it carefully. If you choose not to do that activity, skip this one, too.

'Help Pupils Stop' returns to the questions in 'Help Pupils Understand', with the addition of more questions designed to start pupils thinking about alternatives and solutions. If a pupil has identified one or more 'Reasons Why' as true for him or her, you can refer to 'Reasons Why (Guidance Questions)' (pages 143–144) for ideas on where to go next.

Important:
The 'Guidance Questions' aren't meant to be comprehensive or conclusive, and you'll notice they don't have 'the answers'. Read them, think about them, then add your own notes and ideas. Be sure to consult your SENCO or educational psychologist; he or she will be a valuable resource.

STARTER TIPS FOR HELPING THEM STOP

A few possibilities to consider:

- Pair each pupil with a partner – an older pupil he or she respects, admires and would like to be friends with. The older pupil can offer advice, just listen, and monitor the younger pupil's behaviour (speech, actions, body language etc.). The older pupil can praise positive changes and point out when the younger pupil reverts to bad habits or negative behaviours.

- When a pupil commits to making a change, suggest the 'one-day-at-a-time' approach rather than a blanket promise for the future. *Example*: Instead of "I'll never pick on anyone ever again," try "I won't pick on anyone today."

---

* See 'Change Their Thinking' (pages 125–126).

- If possible, have pupils apologise and make amends to their former targets. Have them keep trying, even if the former targets are suspicious or don't believe the pupils are serious.

- Pair pupils with newcomers to your classroom or school. The newcomers won't know about the pupils' past, which will help clear the way for a possible friendship.

- Help pupils find and pursue interests outside of school and away from their former targets (and reputations). Encourage them to make new friends.

- Help pupils find and pursue physical sports or disciplines (cycling, skating, football) as a way to let off steam and use their strength in positive ways.

- Try to form a 'safety net' of adults (teachers, teaching assistants, MSAs, playground supervisors, dining hall supervisors) the pupils can go to when you're not available. These people should know that the pupils have had behaviour problems and sincerely want to change. The pupils can go to their 'safety net' people when they feel angry, upset or about to lose control.

You know that you sometimes bully other people. Have you ever wondered why? When we know the reasons for our behaviours, this can give us the power to change our behaviours.

Maybe one or more of these reasons are true for you. Read them, think about them and decide for yourself. Write answers only if you want to.

1.   Is there someone in your life who picks on you?

2.   Do you feel lonely at school?

3.   Are you afraid of being picked on?

4.   When other people hurt you, do you feel you have to get back at them?

5.   Do you feel you have to prove that you're tougher and stronger than other people?

6.   Do you just like to show off and get a reaction? Do you like lots of attention?

7.   Do you always have to win at everything? Do you get angry when you lose?

8.   Are you jealous of other people?

9.   Is there someone who irritates you so much you just can't stand it?

10.   When you say or do something to hurt someone else, does that make you feel strong and important?

11.   Is there something in your life that makes you feel unhappy or afraid?

CONTINUED

12. When you feel sad, frustrated, angry or afraid, does it seem that the only way to get rid of your bad feeling is to take it out on someone else?

13. Is there something in your life that makes you feel angry much of the time?

14. Is school really hard for you?

15. Do you feel that you're always letting other people down?
    Are their expectations just too high?

16. Are you bigger and stronger than other people your age?
    Does this make you feel powerful?

17. Do you hang around with other bullies? Do you feel you have to go along with whatever they do?

18. Is it very hard for you to control your temper? Does it seem impossible sometimes?

One more thing to think about . . .

Is there an adult you trust and respect – someone you think you could talk to? Would you be willing to talk to that person? OR: If you can't think of anyone, would you be willing to meet someone who's a really good listener?

1. Is there someone in your life who picks on you?

   Go further: Do you want to tell me who it is? Would you like me to help you do something about it?

2. Do you feel lonely at school?

   Go further: Would you like to feel less lonely and more like you belong here? Are you willing to try some ideas for fitting in?

3. Are you afraid of being picked on?

   Go further: Do you feel the only way to protect yourself is to get other people before they get you? Would you like to learn other ways to feel safe and not worry so much?

4. When other people hurt you, do you feel you have to get back at them?

   Go further: Would you like to learn other ways to deal with the hurt? And maybe avoid feeling hurt? Is it possible that people aren't hurting you on purpose?

5. Do you feel you have to prove that you're tougher and stronger than other people?

   Go further: Are you willing to try other ways to feel powerful and important?

6. Do you just like to show off and get a reaction? Do you like lots of attention?

   Go further: If you knew other ways to get attention – positive ways – would you try them?

7. Do you always have to win at everything? Do you get angry when you lose?

   Go further: Would you like to learn how to enjoy things more and not worry so much about winning or losing?

8. Are you jealous of other people?

   Go further: Why are you jealous? What do they have that you want? Is it really that important? Would you like to learn ways to be happy with who you are and what you have?

9. Is there someone who irritates you so much you just can't stand it?

   Go further: Would you like to learn ways to avoid the person – or not let him or her 'get to you' as much?

10. When you say or do something to hurt someone else, does that make you feel strong and important?

    Go further: Are you willing to try other ways to feel good about yourself?

CONTINUED

11. Is there something in your life that makes you feel unhappy or afraid?

    Go further: What would make you feel better? Would you like someone to help you?

12. When you feel sad, frustrated, angry or afraid, does it seem like the only way to get rid of your bad feeling is to take it out on someone else?

    Go further: If you knew other ways to get rid of bad feelings, would you try them instead?

13. Is there something in your life that makes you feel angry much of the time?

    Go further: Would you like to know how to handle your anger – maybe even get rid of some or all of your anger?

14. Is school really hard for you?

    Go further: If you knew ways to make school easier and more fun, would you try them?

15. Do you feel like you're always letting other people down? Are their expectations just too high?

    Go further: Would you like to tell them how you feel? Would you feel better if they backed off a bit and accepted you the way you are?

16. Are you bigger and stronger than other people your age? Does this make you feel powerful?

    Go further: Do you ever wish you weren't so big and strong? Would you like to know positive ways to use your size and strength?

17. Do you hang around with other bullies? Do you feel you have to go along with whatever they do?

    Go further: If you had a chance to get out of that group (or gang), would you?

18. Is it very hard for you to control your temper? Does it seem impossible sometimes?

    Go further: Would you like to learn ways to control your temper, or how to get help when you can't?

Finally . . .

Is there an adult you respect and trust – someone you think you could talk to? Would you be willing to talk to that person? OR: If you can't think of anyone, would you be willing to meet someone who's a really good listener?

Go further: If you know someone and tell me who it is, I can help get the two of you together. Would that be okay? OR: May I suggest someone you might want to meet?

RESOURCES

DCSF PUBLICATIONS RELATING TO BULLYING

Advice on anti-bullying measures, including the following documents, can be found online at:

http://www.teachernet.gov.uk/wholeschool/behaviour/tacklingbullying

Safe to Learn; Embedding Anti-Bullying Work in Schools

Safe to Learn; Embedding Anti-Bullying Work in Schools – Cyberbullying

Cyberbullying Guidance – Summary Leaflet

Safe to Learn; Embedding Anti-Bullying Work in School – Preventing and Responding to Homophobic Bullying in Schools

Bullying – A Charter for Action

BOOKS FOR ADULTS

A Teacher's Guide to 'Stick Up for Yourself' – Every Kid's Guide to Personal Power and Positive Self-esteem

This book provides teachers (and possibly parents/carers) with support, guidance and information for use with 'Stick Up for Yourself – Every Kid's Guide to Personal Power'.

Author: Gershen Kaufman

Publisher: Free Spirit Publishing Inc., US; Rev Upd edition (2000)

ISBN: 978-1575420691

The Anti-Bullying Handbook

The Anti-Bullying Handbook is a comprehensive resource for parents, teachers, SENCOs and anyone who works with children. It explains simply and clearly what bullying is. It also outlines how to approach setting up a whole school anti-bullying programme, how to deal with bullying as it occurs, and how to ensure it doesn't happen again. The book also identifies and describes the best anti-bullying sites from the Internet.

Author: Keith Sullivan

Publisher: OUP Australia and New Zealand (2000)

ISBN: 978-0195583885

Beyond Bullying: A Guide for Coping After Bullying

Self-help guide for confidence building and coping after bullying. Ages 14–25.

Authors: Howard Martin, Gaby Shenton, Cath Bracher-Giles

Publisher: Kidscape (1999)

ISBN: 978-1872572062

Bullying in Schools: How Successful Can Interventions Be?

This book takes a look at the different approaches in tackling bullying through studying a variety of anti-bullying programmes from around the world and comparing how effective each one is. It looks at the actual procedures and processes as well as the outcomes and critically assesses the reasons for success or failure.

Authors: Peter K. Smith (Editor), Debra Pepler (Editor), Ken Rigby (Editor)

Publisher: Cambridge University Press (2004)

ISBN: 978-0521528030

Dealing with Bullying in Schools: A Training Manual for Teachers, Parents and Other Professionals

This book is a training manual that aims to meet the needs of the class teacher, the school management team, the bullied, the bullies and the parents of both parties. Each chapter offers a set of resources with commentaries for these different groups, so that the reader is provided with a complete pack of advice, guidance and resources. The book includes: a step-by-step guide to formulating an anti-bullying policy for your school; suggested strategies for countering and preventing bullying; detailed advice on working with parents; clear guidance for parents on what to do if their child is being bullied or is doing the bullying.

Authors: Mona O'Moore, Stephen James Minton

Publisher: Paul Chapman Educational Publishing (2004)

ISBN: 978-1412902816

The Bully, the Bullied and the Bystander: From Preschool to Secondary School – How Parents and Teachers Can Help Break the Cycle of Violence

This book provides information and guidance to parents and teachers about different types of bullying, skills that can help prevent a child from becoming a target of bullying, what to do if your child is a bully, how to help a bullied child recover, how to discipline the bully, how to evaluate the effectiveness of your anti-bullying policy and more.

Author: Barbara Coloroso

Publisher: Piccadilly Press Ltd; New edition (2005)

ISBN: 978-1853408472

When Your Child Is Bullied

This book offers advice and reassurance for the parents/carers of bullied children. It is full of ideas about making communication and family life more positive to help everyone recover from the experience of bullying.

Author: Jenny Alexander

Publisher: Pocket Books (2006)

ISBN: 978-1416522355

101 Ways to Deal with Bullying: A Guide for Parents

If you are the parent of a bully or the parent of a child who is being bullied, this book provides you with sensible, practical advice on how to handle bullying – however severe. It includes chapters on the signs and symptoms of bullying, guidance on how to help the targets and the bullies, how to discuss bullying with your child's teacher, the law relating to bullying and more.

Author: Michele Elliot

Publisher: Hodder Mobius (1997)

ISBN: 978-0340695197

BOOKS FOR CHILDREN

NON-FICTION

Bullies Are a Pain in the Brain

This book is a comprehensive guide that aims to help children deal with bullying. It includes cartoon-like illustrations that teach children (and adults) about bullies, how to deal with them and how to remain safe.

Author: Trevor Romain

Publisher: Free Spirit Publishing Inc., US (1997)

ISBN: 978-1575420233

Bullies, Bigmouths and So-called Friends

This easy-to-read book would suit 8–18-year-olds but would also be useful for teachers addressing the issue of bullying with their class or for use in assemblies. It includes advice, fictional case studies, self-esteem strategies and useful phone numbers, websites and addresses.

Author: Jenny Alexander

Publisher: Hodder Children's Books; New edition (2006)

ISBN: 978-0340911846

Don't Pick on Me: How to Handle Bullying

This book offers practical advice for children on how to handle bullying by using fictional scenarios. It explores why some people bully, why others are bullied and what you can do to change things.

Author: Rosemary Stones

Publisher: Piccadilly Press Ltd; New edition (2005)

ISBN: 978-1853408021

Feeling Happy, Feeling Safe

This picture book is a tool that can be used by parents/carers to teach children under six about getting lost, bullying and other difficult experiences in life.

Author: Michele Elliott

Publisher: Hodder Children's Books (1991)

ISBN: 978-0340553862

Hot Stuff to Help Kids Chill Out: The Anger Management Book

This book aims to help children with anger management. It is written in an easy-to-understand way and includes looking at what anger is, exploring it and useful strategies for dealing with it.

Author: Jerry Wilde

Publisher: LGR Publishing (1997)

ISBN: 978-0965761000

How to Handle Bullies, Teasers and Other Meanies

This comprehensive book includes practical strategies that will help children become more assertive and less likely to become targets of bullying.

Author: Kate Cohen-Posey

Publisher: Rainbow Books (1995)

ISBN: 978-1568250298

I Feel Bullied (Your Feelings)

Aimed at children aged seven and under, this book helps children to empathise with a target of bullying. It also looks at different types of bullying and how to deal with them.

Author: Jen Green

Publisher: Hodder Wayland; New edition (1999)

ISBN: 978-0750225762

First Look at Bullying: Stop Picking on Me (A First Look at...)

This book looks at the causes and the effects of both physical and verbal bullying and encourages communication of fears and worries to those that can help.

Author: Pat Thomas

Publisher: Hodder Wayland; New edition (2000)

ISBN: 978-0750028875

Help Hope Happiness

A 9-year-old author's tried and tested strategies for coping with the challenges life can send us. It is an ideal prompt for discussion between parents/carers and their children.

Author: Libby Rees

Publisher: Aultbea Publishing Company (2005)

ISBN: 978-1905517022

Stick Up for Yourself: Every Kid's Guide to Personal Power and Self-Esteem

This book, aimed at older children, looks at solving problems, your feelings, responsibility, making choices and learning to like yourself. It uses short stories to illustrate these issues and can be used to aid conversations between parents/carers and their children.

Author: Gershen Kaufman

Publisher: Free Spirit Publishing Inc., US; Rev. and Updated edition (1999)

ISBN: 978-1568250298

A Bully Picked on Me (It Happened to Me)

This book describes in a realistic and honest way what it is like for a young child to be bullied. The simple story of the arrival of a bully at school is told from a child's point of view, letting young readers know they are not alone. Designed for adults and children to read together or for older children to read by themselves, the book acknowledges children's distress and emphasises to them the importance of talking to others about how they are feeling.

Authors: Elizabeth O'Loughlin, Adam Blackledge

Publisher: Pangolin Books (2005)

ISBN: 978-1844930197

A Volcano in My Tummy:
Helping Children to Handle Anger

This book presents a clear and effective approach to helping children and adults alike understand and deal constructively with children's anger. The book offers engaging, well-organised activities which help to overcome the fear of children's anger that many adult care-givers experience, and distinguishes between anger the feeling, and violence the behaviour. Primarily created for ages 6 to 13, it is accessible for use in class or at home.

Author: Eliane Whitehouse

Publisher: New Society Publishers (1997)

ISBN: 978-0865713499

Alison and the Bully Monsters

Alison Little is scared of lots of things. Of the dog next door, of the boys down the road, of the bigger girls – of her own shadow, you might say! This is a story of courage and triumph.

Author: Jac Jones

Publisher: Pont Books (2000)

ISBN: 978-1859027523

Bad Girls

This book deals lightly but sensitively with the terrible pain suffered by a ten-year-old girl when she becomes the target of vicious bullying at school. When the over-protected, intelligent Mandy is cast out by her so-called girl 'friends' at school, she takes up with the trendy, cheerful 14-year-old Tanya. Because Mandy reminds Tanya of her much-loved kid sister in care, and because she too is lonely, the two quickly become best friends. But Tanya's unhappy life has made her turn to petty crime and before long Mandy finds herself in deep water.

Suggested age range: 9–12

Author: Jacqueline Wilson

Publisher: Corgi Yearling Books; New edition (2006)

ISBN: 978-0440867623

Chicken

Suitable for 9–12-year-olds, this is a powerful and humorous story about a family on the theme of bullying. Davy's too chicken to stand up to bullying at school. He's been singled out as an easy target. His family aren't much help - they're all chicken too. Mum's frightened of learning to drive, big brother Carl is terrifying himself trying to impress his new friends. And Dad has too many problems of his own to be sympathetic. But in the end it's his little sister's strange secret which spurs Davy on... and surprises the whole family as well.

Author: Alan Gibbons

Publisher: Orion Children's Books; New edition (1994)

ISBN: 978-1858810515

Cloud Busting

Despite his mum's insistence, Sam doesn't want to be friends with Davey; he thinks Davey's a first class, grade A, top of the dung heap moron. But one day Davey saves Sam's life and a bond is formed between them. Sam is still embarrassed to be seen with Davey, but little by little he has to admit, when it's just the two of them, Davey is a lot of fun. But then something terrible happens to Davey. Told in verse, in the first person, this is the touching story of an extraordinary friendship that changes two boys' lives forever. Suitable for ages 8 and above.

Author: Malorie Blackman

Publisher: Corgi Yearling Books; New edition (2005)

ISBN: 978-0440866152

Don't Be a Bully, Billy! (Cautionary Tales)

This story is designed to introduce very young children to the idea of right and wrong. Each central character discovers in an amusing way the penalty of ignoring warnings to behave properly. It helps to teach children about the consequences of their actions.

Authors: J. McCaferty, Phil Roxbee Cox

Publisher: Usborne Publishing Ltd (2004)

ISBN: 978-0746052747

Driftwood

Hannah has been best friends with Joey forever. When Joey acquires a foster brother, Paul, and then falls in love with Hannah's big brother, the dynamics of their relationship begin to change and Hannah finds it hard to adjust. At the same time, she discovers that not only is Paul being bullied mercilessly at school because he is 'different', but it is her own brother who is doing the bullying. When Paul goes missing, the police become involved and everyone's secrets come out into the open. Tackles a number of serious issues in a humorous and accessible fashion that will appeal to both boys and girls. Suitable for 9–14-year-olds.

Author: Cathy Cassidy

Publisher: Puffin Books (2005)

ISBN: 978-0141320212

Finding Fizz

A story about bullying and being 'one of the gang'. Carly hasn't been herself lately – it seems that she's 'lost her fizz'. She is being teased and excluded by the girls who were once her best friends, and feels there is no one she can talk to about her problems. Then Carly finds a stray dog that needs a home.

Author: Jen Alexander

Publisher: A&C Black (2006)

ISBN: 978-0713676259

Hope and the Bullies: The Girl Who Drew the Line at Bullying

A picture book for children of seven to nine years, this innovative and artistic book allows for discussion around bullying and how we treat one another. It is ideal for groups with poor literacy skills – and can be a trigger to develop artwork and posters in the classroom. Includes a resources list for children.

Author: Louise Alexander

Publisher: Young Voice (2004)

ISBN: 978-1903456163

Indigo's Star

This is a moving novel about the Casson family and in particular the plight of a boy called Indigo. It tackles the issue of bullying effectively using humour. It also tackles other relationship issues. It is a story of survival.

Author: Hilary McKay

Publisher: Hodder Children's Books; New edition (2004)

ISBN: 978-0340875797

Inventing Elliot

Elliot was bullied at his old school so sees making a fresh start at a new school as an opportunity to avoid bullying by being the exact opposite of what he was. He tries to be as average as possible (except for excelling at swimming) to avoid any attention.

Unfortunately his plan does not work and his behaviour results in him gaining the status of ringleader for a gang of bullies. Elliot ends up in a state of emotional turmoil and faces many dilemmas.

Author: Graham Gardner

Publisher: Orion Children's Books (2004)

ISBN: 978-1842552087

Run Zan Run

Katie is bullied but no one believes her. During one bullying incident a mysterious girl called Zan rushes to her defence. Zan is unwilling to talk to Katie and wants her identity to remain secret. But slowly Katie learns the truth about Zan, and when she does, she realises Zan has much more to lose than the safety of her cardboard box. A gripping story that really brings the issue of bullying to a head.

Author: Catherine MacPhail

Publisher: Bloomsbury (2005)

ISBN: 978-0747578345

The Angel of Nitshill Road

Until the angel (Angelica – a new pupil) came, Penny, Mark and Marigold were bitterly unhappy. 'Fat.' 'Freak.' 'Smelly.' Barry Hunter was bullying them and everyone at Nitshill Road School knew it. But the angel brings a clever solution. Life at school is going to be very different from now on.

Author: Anne Fine

Publisher: Egmont Books Ltd (2007)

ISBN: 978-1405233200

The Great Harlequin Grim

Glenn Jackson has just moved to an isolated village in the Lake District with his father after the separation of his parents. He has no friends and only his love of art to keep him going. His status as an outsider means he is bullied. The story evolves when Glenn meets the simple Harlequin Grim, who fends for himself on the hills. This

story explores the issues of prejudice, loss and love. Suitable for children aged 11 and over.

Author: Gareth Thompson

Publisher: Doubleday (2006)

ISBN: 978-0385609203

The Huge Bag of Worries

This book, aimed at younger children, explores the idea that keeping worries to yourself is not a healthy thing to do. Told through the story of a little girl called Jenny who carries her worries around with her (in a bag) that she just cannot get rid of on her own, she eventually encounters a lady who helps her to understand how to sort it all out!

Author: Virginia Ironside

Publisher: Hodder Children's Books (2004)

ISBN: 978-0340903179

The Present Takers

Melanie Prosser and her gang have the school sewn up. Every time it's another girl's birthday they have ways of getting what they want – and the ways hurt. But Lucy, the latest target, knows she should fight back and she's going to need all the help she can get. Suitable for 13+.

Author: Aidan Chambers

Publisher: Red Fox; New edition (1994)

ISBN: 978-0099991601

What's Your Problem?

A powerful novel aimed at teenagers that follows the teenage boy Jaspal's move from Leicester to rural Nottinghamshire for a 'better life'. However, Jaspal experiences racial abuse, prejudice, hate mail and threats at his new home.

Author: Sherry Ashworth

Publisher: Livewire Books for Teenagers (2000)

ISBN: 978-0704349612

Willow Street Kids – Be Smart, Stay Safe

This tale involving the Willow Street Kids is based on a real bullying story. It offers advice on how to deal with such a situation. Suitable for 7–11-year-olds.

Author: Michele Elliott

Publisher: Macmillan Children's Books (1997)

ISBN: 978-0330351843

Willow Street Kids - Beat the Bullies

The Willow Street Kids move to secondary school and run into bullies they knew from primary school. Find out how they beat the bullies. Ages 7–11.

Author: Michele Elliott

Publisher: Macmillan Children's Books (1997)

ISBN: 978-0330351850

Willy the Champ

Willy is different, which means he comes in for a lot of hard times and bullying. Willy likes to read and listen to music. However hard he tries he just cannot get interested in football or swimming, so when Willy meets Buster Nose he is in for a surprise. This book examines the way bullies behave and shows ways of dealing with them.

Author: Anthony Browne

Publisher: Walker Books Ltd; New edition (1996)

ISBN: 978-0744543568

VIDEOS AND DVDS

Bully Free DVD from Kidscape

The DVD makes it easy for teachers and carers to help keep their charges safe for life. Some added extras: interactive menu options that allow the viewer to navigate and select different scenes for practice and review, instant playback by scene or chapter, subtitles option.

Available from the Kidscape website: www.kidscape.org.uk

It Shouldn't Happen!

DVD, guide and notes for teaching younger people how to stay safe from bullying. It contains role-plays, verbal assertiveness exercises and a range of techniques to keep safe from bullies. With an interactive menu to simplify navigation and subtitles for those with hearing impairments. Ages 7–11.

Available from the Kidscape website: www.kidscape.org.uk

Sticks and Stones Video

For teens, realistic bullying incidents and role-plays. Good for discussion.

Available from the Kidscape website: www.kidscape.org.uk

Why Bullies Win

'Why Bullies Win' explores why, with so many initiatives and millions of pounds spent on campaigns, many children still have nowhere to turn. Copies of this programme are available – send an email to panorama@bbc.co.uk with the subject 'Why bullies win video' and you'll be advised how to obtain a copy at cost price.

BBC 1 Panorama: http://news.bbc.co.uk/1/hi/programmes/panorama/4241795.stm

ORGANISATIONS

Anti-Bullying Alliance

The Anti-Bullying Alliance (ABA) was founded by the NSPCC and the National Children's Bureau in 2002. It is hosted and supported by NCB. The Alliance brings together more than 65 organisations into one network with the aim of reducing bullying and creating safer environments in which children and young people can live, grow, play and learn.

email: aba@ncb.org.uk

address: ABA, National Children's Bureau, 8 Wakley Street, London, EC1V 7QE

website: www.anti-bullyingalliance.org.uk

Beat Bullying

Aims to reduce and prevent the incidence and impact of bullying by devising anti-bullying strategies for young people by young people.

tel: 0845 338 5060

website: www.beatbullying.org

British Association of Anger Management

A professional body of consultants, counsellors and trainers that offer support, programmes and training for the general public, children and teenagers, the educational sector and anyone dealing with their own or another's anger.

tel: 0845 1300 286

website: www.angermanage.co.uk

Bully Free Zone

Provides a peer mediation service, written and telephone advice, and provides training for children and young people, parents, teachers, youth workers and other professionals.

tel: 01204 454958

website: www.bullyfreezone.co.uk

Bullying UK

Formerly known as Bullying Online, Bullying UK is an anti-bullying charity providing support for parents, teachers and children. Particular expertise in online issues.

website: www.bullying.co.uk

Childline

ChildLine is the UK's free national helpline for children and young people in trouble or danger, who can call free 24 hours a day on:

freephone: 0800 1111

website: www.childline.org.uk

Children's Legal Centre

Provides legal advice, information, assistance and representation to children, parents/carers and professionals working with children.

tel: 01206 872466

Young People's freephone: 0800 7832187

website: www.childrenslegalcentre.com

Commission for Racial Equality

A publicly funded, non-governmental body set up under the Race Relations Act 1976 to tackle racial discrimination and promote racial equality.

tel: 020 7939 0000

website: www.cre.gov.uk

Diana Princess of Wales Memorial Award for Young People

The Diana Anti-bullying Award is open to primary schools, secondary schools and youth organisations.

tel: 0845 3372987

website: www.diana-award.org.uk

Educational Action Challenging Homophobia (EACH)

Established to challenge homophobia in education.

tel: 0808 1000143

website: www.eachaction.org.uk

Education for All

Joint campaign by Stonewall, Fflag and LGBT Youth Scotland to combat homophobic bullying. Website includes resources, research and case studies.

tel: 020 7593 1851

website: www.stonewall.org.uk/education_for_all

Kidscape

The support available from Kidscape includes:

A helpline for parents/carers of children who are being bullied: 08451 205204

Booklets, Literature, Posters, Training Guides, Educational Videos on bullying, child protection, and parenting

National Comprehensive Training Programme on child safety and behaviour management issues

Confidence-building session for children who have been bullied

Kidscape, 2 Grosvenor Gardens, London, SW1W 0DH.

tel: 020 7730 3300 fax: 020 7730 7081

website: www.kidscape.org.uk

Leap Confronting Conflict

Leap is a national voluntary youth organisation and registered charity that provides opportunities, regionally and nationally, for young people and adults to explore creative approaches to conflict in their lives.

tel: 0207 272 5630

website: www.leaplinx.com

Mencap

Mencap fights for equal rights for people with learning disabilities and their families and carers, and provides housing and employment support.

tel: 020 7454 0454

website: www.mencap.org.uk

National Children's Bureau

Promotes the voices, interests and well-being of all children and young people across every aspect of their lives. As an umbrella body for the children's sector in England and Northern Ireland, provides information on policy, research and best practice.

tel: 020 7843 6000

website: www.ncb.org.uk

NSPCC

The NSPCC is a registered charity that aims to end cruelty to children. Works with children and families, as well as influencing the public with campaigns, policy and attitudes.

tel: 0207 825 2500

website: www.nspcc.org.uk

NSPCC — National Child Protection Helpline

A 24-hour helpline for anyone concerned about a child at risk of abuse (including bullying) and including children themselves.

freephone 0800 800 500

Samaritans

Samaritans provides confidential non-judgmental emotional support 24 hours a day for people who are experiencing feelings of distress or despair, including those which could lead to suicide. Also offers an email service.

helpline: 0117 983 1000

Scottish Anti-Bullying Network

The Anti-Bullying Network was established to provide free support for anti-bullying work in schools. Its website provides information about bullying and how it can be tackled. It also operates an anti-bullying service which will include the provision of training, publications and consultancy services.

website: www.antibullying.net

address: The Anti-Bullying Network, Simpson House, 52 Queen Street, Edinburgh, EH2 3NS

email: info@antibullying.net

SupportLine

Offers confidential emotional support to children, young adults and adults by telephone, email and post. Works with callers to develop healthy, positive coping strategies, an inner feeling of strength and increased self-esteem. They also keep details of counsellors, agencies and support groups throughout the UK.

tel: 020 8554 9004

email: info@supportline.org.uk

website: www.supportline.org.uk

Teacher Support Network

An independent charity that provides practical and emotional support for teachers and their families.

address: Hamilton House, Mabledon Place, London WC1H 9BE

tel: 020 7554 5200

email: enquiries@teachersupport.info

website: www.teachersupport.org.uk

Teachers TV

Section of the Teachers TV website devoted to anti-bullying, featuring programmes which can be watched online, downloadable resources, links, and interviews with experts on bullying.

website: www.teachers.tv/bullying

The Advisory Centre for Education

A charity that offers free advice for parents and carers on a variety of aspects to do with education. It also offers a variety of helpful publications.

general advice line: (Mon–Fri 10 am–5 pm) 0808 800 5793

Young Minds

A children's mental health charity that also runs a parents'/carers' information service for anyone concerned about the mental health of a young person:

tel: 0800 018 2138

website: www.youngminds.org.uk

INDEX